Animal Totems and Spirit Guides: The Wisdom of Owl

Second Edition

Jordana Van

DEDICATION

For Shawn Van, Kris Shubin, Bridgette Valeron, Heather Jacobs, and Mike Buchta. You probably didn't know this, but in moments of doubt, at least one of you appears in my imagination dressed as a cheerleader waving pom-poms and belting out a rousing fight-song. And you all look great in a skirt.

CONTENTS

ACKNOWLEDGEMENTS AND
AUTHOR'S NOTE

One of the many perks of doing the work that I do is variety; one day I may speak with someone in the United States, the next with someone in Mozambique, the next in South Korea, and then Croatia, New Zealand, Sweden, Brazil, Germany, and Saudi Arabia in the days that follow. My clients are young and old; gay, straight, bisexual, and transgender; wealthy, middle-class, and still searching for their means to prosperity; married, single, dating, experimenting, divorced, and widowed; of all educational backgrounds and in a mind-boggling assortment of careers; and of all faiths, including those who consider themselves atheists, and those still seeking something bigger than themselves in which to believe. It is largely through this outstanding collection of individuals from such different circumstances that my understanding of the way in which Owl functions as a totem and a spirit guide has been developed and refined, and more, that I have come to see

Owl as a shining example of our inherent Oneness. Through my work with Owl, it has become strikingly apparent that the frustrations and failures, self-doubts and fears, obsessions and confusions and episodes of sudden, inexplicable Knowing that so many of us believe must be unique to us alone are in fact being experienced by our brothers and sisters both in the home next door and on the other side of the world. After speaking with hundreds of Owl People, no other totem has proven to be more universal, and in fact, it is precisely because so many Owl People have found their way into my life that the need for a second, more thorough edition of this book became so rapidly apparent!

To all of those with whom I have spoken about Owl, and to all of those in the future, this book is both *for* you and exists because *of* you. Thank you for sharing your experiences and your understandings, and for asking the kind of complicated, mind-bending questions that only Owl People can ask! A brain cell or a thousand might have died of exhaustion while attempting to discern the answers, but they died satisfied!

Specific thanks also goes to the following individuals: To my husband, Shawn, if you were only there to extricate me from some technological mayhem or other every time I screamed (a daily—if not hourly—chore), I would consider myself beyond blessed. But you have also been my anchor, my best friend, my unwavering supporter, and have always known exactly when to leave me alone, and when to show me a photo of a kitten to snap me out of a cranky spell. I love you, I love you, I love you. To my artist-Mama, thank you for creating the beautiful new book cover, for sharing my enthusiasm over all things furred and feathered (and occasionally scaled and creepy), for being your ever-intriguing Owl Woman Self, and for your continued love and encouragement. To Samuel Jones, thank you for being a much-needed source of perspective and validation, for all of your incredible insights, and for your friendship. I'm not quite sure how I functioned before I met you! Jamie Montey, for asking me that question about Duck, I will be forever grateful. And to the divine Burrowline, who has not only donated her time and expertise in the creation of French subtitles for my *Animal Totems and Spirit Guides* series of videos on YouTube, but provided a much needed insider's perspective on Burrowing Owl—complete with a series of perfectly chosen photographs and videos that kept me laughing along the way—thank you for being the thorough, thoughtful, loving, and spectacularly funny soul that you are. You are an absolute treasure.

JORDANA VAN

1 HOW TO USE THIS BOOK

While this book was written especially for those of you who have always felt a special bond with owls, and those for whom Owls[1] are suddenly making a dramatic or frequent appearance, it is also an all-purpose introduction to the extraordinary world of animal totems and spirit guides as a whole, a world that you may have previously perceived as inaccessible, incomprehensible, or just plain imaginary. Even if you have never recognized it before, all of those strange animal experiences really *were* intended to communicate something important, nor is it wishful thinking that what you feel for these creatures goes beyond mere appreciation for their unique qualities. You do not need to be in the midst of a trance or meditation to receive

---

[1] "Owl" with a capital "O" refers to the animal as a totem and/or spirit guide, or to a person with this totem, while a lowercase "o" denotes the earthly creature. These are not always mutually exclusive, and in those cases, a capital "O" is used.

guidance from your totems and/or spirit guides, nor do you have to complete a lengthy or complicated ritual; instead, it is my experience that anyone—even spiritual "laypeople" who never engage in any of the aforementioned practices—can access this wisdom *all of the time* simply by being aware and open-minded.

In the section devoted to understanding animal totems and spirit guides, you will learn not only what these things are and how to identify them, but several methods that you can use to easily connect with yours. I have employed each of these methods successfully myself, though the more I strive to move from a purely intuitive place, the less I find myself relying upon a specific method to obtain assistance. If I need animal guidance, it arrives without my asking, though this does not always mean that I recognize it when it appears! Sometimes, the messages are *so* obvious, and *so* perfect, that the part of ourselves that still believes that some effort must be exerted in exchange for guidance often overlooks it completely! Given that the art of working with our animal totems and spirit guides is more often about interpreting smaller, more everyday experiences (that we can easily rationalize away, if we are not used to trusting guidance from this quarter) than the dramatic, so over-the-top-they-can't-be-denied sort of happenings, I have also included a chapter detailing an incident from my own life in which a spirit guide appeared over and over in a multitude of ways, and I simply could not figure out what it meant—both because I had a limited view of the problem, and because the message was so obvious that I overlooked it.

In the chapter devoted to Owl as a totem, you will find not only a discussion of the Owl Person's typical personality type, but a thorough exploration of the challenges Owl People experience during their lifetime and what they can do to resolve these challenges in a way that leads them to increased joy and fulfillment on all levels. Spiritual growth, after all, is not merely about improving one's understanding of oneself and developing a greater appreciation of one's own unique soul, but learning how to put this new love to use creating a life that reflects this appreciation. When we love ourselves, we naturally look and feel better, work in careers that are more fulfilling and meet our financial needs, attract loving relationships, and have a great deal more fun!

In the chapter devoted to Owl as a spirit guide, you will find a thorough list of the messages that are attached to the appearance of Owls in one's life. When combined with an honest assessment of your current situation—whether this involves your physical or mental health, spirituality, finances, relationships, creative endeavors, or any other concern—these messages tell you precisely how to realign with your most authentic, balanced self. From this place, decisions are made more easily, trials resolve more quickly, and circumstances that may previously have been viewed as insurmountable mountains dwindle into mole-hills.

In the chapter devoted to species-specific wisdom, you will find additional details pertaining to the eight owls about which I am asked most often: barn owl, barred owl, burrowing owl, Eurasian eagle owl, great grey owl, great horned owl, great snowy owl, and screech owl. If you identify not just with owls in general, but with one of these *specific* owls, the additional details they offer may assist you to interpret Owl's presence in your life with greater clarity.

This information is intended to be used in tandem with the information on Owl in general, which appears in the preceding chapters.

In this new edition, I have also chosen to include a chapter that answers one of my most frequently received questions: "What does it mean when I dream about owls?" In addition to interpreting Owl as a dream-symbol, this chapter provides a basic understanding of dream interpretation, which is intended to assist you in making the best possible use of your dreams, whether they include owls or not.

This text concludes with a chapter that features a description of one of the many ways in which Owl has made an appearance in my own life, so that you may have a reference to use in interpreting your own experiences. Your own encounters with Owl may be similar, or they may be very different, but they will always be meaningful.

Owl is the seeker of pure Truth above all—the truth of ourselves, the truth of others, the truth of the world around us. Small daily truths, large cosmic ones . . . nothing is excluded. To fully connect with Owl is to strip away all deception and denial, to look into the shadows within and the shadows without, and to meet what is discovered there with an open mind and an open heart. Thus do we become torchbearers, beacons of truth and love guiding those still stumbling through the darkness in which we, too, once were lost.

I wish you ease and joy as you set foot upon this path.

2 UNDERSTANDING ANIMAL TOTEMS AND SPIRIT GUIDES

What is an Animal Totem?

An animal[2] totem can be an actual spirit sent by our guides to assist us, a vision or idea provided by our Higher Selves, or a combination thereof. It can appear in a concrete form that we physically see and experience (whether this is in "real life" or through a work of art, a photograph, or a recording); we may discover it through a song or words on a page; it can come to us in a vision or a dream; or we may simply "know" that it is there. One's totem can be any organism in physical or mythological existence, even one that is considered to be fantastical in nature, such as a dragon, unicorn, or griffin. Another human being would not be considered a totem, however, nor would a faerie, mermaid, or similar humanoid spirit.

---

[2] For the sake of simplicity, I use the word "animal" or "creature" to represent all totem creatures, including animals, insects, plants, and mythological beasts.

What is the Purpose of a Totem?

A totem is a bit like a magic mirror. When we recognize it and make the decision to work with it, it shows us our reflection. Certain parts of ourselves will be met with approval, and others will make us want to look away. But the mirror also reveals the who we *could* be, the person we would perceive as perfect because our present flaws have either been reframed or released. We may have rejected pieces of ourselves simply because others said that we should, and our totem would show us that not only are those pieces quite beautiful, but that they are worthy of our love. Or, we may be shown that something we did not like about ourselves was not actually a part of *ourselves* at all, but a defense-mechanism that could be surrendered, or a physical or emotional ailment that could be healed.

If we choose to face our present reflection, our totem will show us how to attain this potential self. This most often occurs through bringing us face-to-face with our stumbling blocks, the challenges we encounter again and again because we possess limiting beliefs about ourselves and our world. When we are able to identify these blocks and understand how and why we have created them, we gain the power to release them. Someone with an Owl totem, for example, will tend to have an easy time deciphering the inner-workings of others and take great joy in doing so; other people fascinate them endlessly! However, they often struggle with shining the same light upon themselves, and so are frequently confused about their emotions and why they feel the way that they do. Because they do not understand their feelings, they have a difficult time identifying what they actually *need*, and so can become caught up in doing things or staying in relationships because they make *sense,* but that don't fulfill them or that actually make them ill. Part of an Owl Person's journey is to learn how to observe their own inner-workings as keenly as they do others', and to discover how to flow with their emotions rather than feel buffeted by them. When they do this, they are more likely to be able to put themselves in circumstances that will benefit them. In this way, a totem not only resonates with key aspects of a person's personality and the manner in which the person tends to approach his or her life, but it also provides the means for shedding one's old, limiting beliefs, and becoming the best and happiest version of oneself that one can be. A totem outlines both the problem *and* the solution!

Depending upon the totem with which we are working at the time, the mirror will show us a different reflection of ourselves and a different potential reflection. With one totem, we may be looking at ourselves as the mother/father/nurturer, and with another, we see ourselves as the lover. One totem may show us the self that goes to work and pays the bills, another ourselves at play, another the self who has difficulty with public speaking. And so someone working with Snake is going to experience a very different journey than someone working with Hummingbird or with Wolf.

Years may be spent upon a single facet of ourselves, during which time that totem will feel closest to us. While we may still be aware of the others, their wisdom will not be as crucial to our forward momentum. It is also possible that we may find ourselves working through multiple challenges at the same time, each with its own totem to provide insight and assistance. We are all unique, and each of us has a different threshold for how much spiritual growth we can handle at once.

Finally, a person will relate more or less strongly to the personality characteristics (and in some cases, the physical characteristics) of each of their totems depending on the lesson(s) with which they are working at the time. This is why one may have more of an Owl personality during one portion of one's life, and more of a Fox personality during another. If one is being assisted by multiple totems at a certain time, one may exhibit select personality traits from each. One does not stop being a Spider Person, or a Bear or Tiger or Alligator Person, even if one's personality experiences a dramatic transformation; rather, one may simply have sufficiently mastered what their totem had to teach them during a crucial point in their life, and they have now moved on to another lesson.

How Many Totems Does Each Person Have?

Although there are numerous belief-systems that offer answers to this question (including the Native American pantheon, which states that we each have nine totems that correspond to positions on the medicine wheel), my personal experience has lead me to steer clear of absolutes. It is my firm belief that whether there is a particular number given to us or not, the greatest growth is accomplished through focusing whole-heartedly on what is occurring for us *In The Now*, rather than concerning ourselves with what may come. Your totems will come to you when you are ready, and not before, and having more is not necessarily better than having fewer. Tell the Universe you are open to their wisdom, cherish each as they arrive, remain open to others, and trust that you are receiving the guidance that is appropriate for you in the way and time that is best. In Chapter Four, I describe my personal methods for making contact with our totems and spirit guides, in case you are at a loss and need some help getting started.

What is a Spirit Guide? Isn't that the Same Thing as a Totem?

Both totems and spirit guides provide us with the wisdom and insight necessary to conquer and eventually dissolve our unique stumbling blocks. The difference is that while our totems are linked with aspects of our personalities and assist us with the most crucial challenges of our lives, spirit guides are more like short-term helpers who show us how to navigate lesser challenges, the equivalent of directing us around a fallen tree versus helping us scale Mount Everest. For example, a spirit guide may assist you with making a financial decision in a way that will benefit you in one specific instance, helping you choose between taking a loan from a bank, asking a relative for money, or applying for a new job. Your totem, on the other hand, will help you learn how to manifest financial wellness throughout your lifetime, guiding you into the career in which you will experience the greatest fulfillment, and teaching you how to open yourself to monetary abundance.

If you are unable to tell whether a creature is one of your totems or is acting as your spirit guide, try asking yourself the following questions:

- First, do the personality characteristics associated with that creature resonate with your own? Do you tend to approach your life and view the world as someone would if that creature were their totem? My books provide a thorough study of the personality characteristics related to each totem, so you may use this information as a reference.

- Second, note the way in which the creature appears and how long it sticks around. If it appears suddenly, you use its wisdom to make the appropriate changes, and then you never see it again (or when you do, the experiences are less frequent and/or intense), it was probably a spirit guide. If, instead, it makes appearances throughout your life, and even after you have begun to do as it counsels, you are still aware of it in a fashion that feels good to you, it is probably a totem.

It is not uncommon for something you first thought was a spirit guide to be revealed as a totem, particularly if you are new to being aware of your environment and using your intuition. You may only now be witnessing evidence of the magic that has always surrounded you, and so while a creature's appearance may seem sudden to you, it may always have been there, and you simply did not notice. On the other hand, you may have had to make some major changes to your life and attitude before you became ready to work with a totem, and so it did not reveal itself in any fashion until you were sufficiently prepared.

So How DO We Discover Our Totems and Spirit Guides? Do We Get to Pick Them Ourselves?

When we genuinely open ourselves to the wisdom of the Universe and allow it to guide us, we often discover that those things that best serve us are not things we would have originally chosen for ourselves, nor even considered at all! So it often is with our animal totems and spirit guides. While many people initially seek to connect with a certain creature on account of its external beauty, perceived power, or prestigious affiliations, these things have nothing whatsoever to do with a creature's wisdom, nor with its ability to guide us. Each creature has its own special wisdom to share, and the only way we can genuinely benefit from communion with our totems and spirit guides is to accept that *we cannot force what is not there nor deny what is!* Persisting in trying to connect with an animal that doesn't resonate with us (For example, trying to force a bond with Beaver because a shaman has told you that Beaver is your totem, but you just don't *feel* it, or insisting that you are a Peacock Person not because you really like Peacocks, but because you believe it will impress others) will yield only frustration and disillusionment, whereas approaching the situation with faith that we will connect with that which serves us best—and welcoming it when it arrives—opens the door to experiences that will enlighten us in ways we never could have imagined.

Fortunately, when we open ourselves to a totem's wisdom, we often develop an affection for it even if none existed before, and sometimes even if all we previously felt was revulsion! Several of my clients who professed an

11

abhorrence of spiders discovered to their enormous shock that when the time arrived to work with Spider as a totem, they were oddly excited and even reveled in being Spider People! In my own case, I never had any particular interest in snakes before Snake revealed itself as a totem, and if someone had told me I was a Snake Person, I would have felt somewhat disappointed. Yet once I began my journey with Snake in earnest, I rapidly discovered that I *liked* Snakes, that I was intrigued by them, and that sightings of them filled me with absolute glee.

There are many different ways to connect with one's totems and guides, some of which involve complicated rituals, an assortment of props, and in a few cases, physical poses, noises, and other animalistic behavior. None of these has ever been necessary to facilitate communication with my own totems and guides, and I would advise that you only engage in these kinds of activities if they resonate with you. The next chapter provides a list of questions to ask yourself to help you identify your totems and/or current spirit guides. If you are still at a loss and are not comfortable simply waiting for the Universe to introduce you to your totem(s), more active approaches have been included in Chapter Four.

Working with totems and spirit guides is not an exact science, and so especially when we are new to this sort of work, it is common to seek the opinion of a third party whom we perceive as being knowledgeable in this arena. There are many wonderful sources of wisdom on this topic, and welcoming someone else's perspective can open our eyes to important things we may have otherwise missed. However, while another person may serve as an earthly guide to assist you in working with your animal totems and spirit guides, it is *only* if this person's analysis resonates with the voice of your heart that it is valid. It is never in your best interests to agree with anything to do with your spirituality just because a spiritual authority tells you that you should. One does *not* have to be a shaman or other spiritual practitioner to access this kind of guidance; one merely has to be open-minded, observant, and willing to approach the task not only with reverence, but with a sense of humor. Sometimes our guides come to us in very serious, intense, and emotional ways, and sometimes they appear in fashions that make us laugh uncontrollably; just because something is hilarious does not make it any less holy, and it will be to your highest good to avoid judging your experiences and just accept them for what they are.

3 IDENTIFYING YOUR ANIMAL TOTEMS AND SPIRIT GUIDES

What follows are some suggestions to aid you in identifying your totem animals, as well as whether a creature is a lifelong totem versus a spirit guide here to help you with a particular situation. All that is required in these cases is awareness and thoughtful reflection. More active approaches are detailed in the next chapter.

A creature is likely to be one of your totems if one or more of the following is true for you, with a greater number of applicable items equaling greater likelihood:

- For as long as you can recall, you have had an interest in this creature.

- Seeing images of this creature or hearing its particular songs, calls, or cries gives you a feeling of comfort, joy, excitement, or unreasonable fear.

- You surround yourself with representations of this creature such as photographs, paintings, drawings, figurines, or other artwork.

- You possess special relics of this creature, such as bones, claws, feathers, or shed skin.

- You wear jewelry or have a tattoo depicting this creature or features of it.

- You read books or enjoy songs about this creature.

- When you need to select a new screen name or password, you use this creature's name.

- People are so aware of your affection for this creature that you frequently find yourself being gifted items having to do with it.

- You have had repeated experiences with this creature throughout your life—even if these are simply frequent sightings—or you have had one or two very intense, very special one-on-one experiences with it.

- The creature is common in your geographic area, yet you always find yourself drawn to it, and you tend to be aware of it before anyone else (For example, our area is heavily populated with hawks, yet I always find myself keenly aware of them when they are present. I also spot them long before my husband, even if we are both facing the same direction!).

- You are afraid of this creature, even when there is no logical reason for this fear, and especially if it is not a creature with which you are likely to come into contact (being afraid of sharks when you don't spend any time in or near the ocean, for example). If this is a creature of which many people are commonly afraid, the degree of fear is important. Someone with a common fear of spiders may jump or shriek when they see one, but someone who has a Spider totem may be so terrified they will have to leave the room until it is removed, and they will be shaken up for hours after.

- You have had a very frightening or traumatic experience with this creature, such as a snake-bite, bear-mauling, or bee-sting causing anaphylactic shock.

- You have had repeated dreams about this creature throughout your life, or you have experienced visions in which this creature—or a figure dressed as this creature—appears.

- Many (though not necessarily all) facets of your personality match the personality characteristics represented by this totem creature.

- Many (though not necessarily all) of the biggest challenges and lessons in your life match those represented by this totem creature.

A creature is likely a spirit guide here to assist you with a particular situation if any of the following items are true for you at this time:

- You have never been especially interested in this creature, yet you suddenly find yourself attracted to photographs, artwork, or jewelry that feature it, or you are suddenly possessed by the desire to get a tattoo depicting it (My advice on this last bit: Don't. This creature may cease to have meaning for you in a month or less! Wait until you know for sure that it is actually a totem before honoring it in permanent ink).

- You are suddenly seeing and/or hearing this creature everywhere. The creature itself may appear to you physically, or you may see or hear it (or something that represents it) through another means such as television, radio, or the Internet. When Bat flew into my life a few years ago, it showed itself not only in the form of live bats that suddenly began swooping in front of my car in the mornings, but as pictures of bats on t-shirts, as well as the Batman logo on a license plate in our neighborhood. It also coincided with several news stories related to the bats that reside in the caves in our area, as well as the release of the last *Batman* movie. All of these things occurred within the space of three days, and Bat wound up heralding the most significant transformation I've experienced in my life to date.

- You are having very intense experiences with this creature, whether these are serene and joyful, frightening, or even traumatic. Common examples may involve an animal approaching you or standing still for a time despite being aware of your presence; allowing you to touch or feed it; running or diving in front of your car; falling out of the sky in front of you; encountering it dead or dying; moving into your home (such as a family of raccoons taking over your attic or wasps making nests under your deck); or even an attack by this creature. If one of your pets is attacked by this creature, it is also likely to be a spirit guide.

- You are having repeated dreams about this creature. This does not *always* mean an animal is your spirit guide, as these creatures have their own dream symbolism in addition to the messages they offer as spirit guides, but if you are dreaming about them *and* you are experiencing them in other ways as well, it is a good indicator that there is some spirit guide wisdom revealing itself to you.

- You are having visions of this creature, or of people dressed like it. These experiences can also be auditory, rather than visual, in which you can hear the creature, but not see it. Hypnogogic experiences that occur just on the cusp of falling asleep or during other times in which you are "zoning out" are also indicators that a spirit guide is trying to get your attention.

- Once you apply this creature's wisdom to your current circumstances and the situation begins to resolve, you cease being interested in it, stop seeing it everywhere, and no longer have noteworthy experiences with it.

4 INTUITIVE METHODS FOR CONNECTING WITH YOUR ANIMAL TOTEMS AND SPIRIT GUIDES

Each of these approaches requires you to be willing to believe that when you ask for guidance, you will receive it. I can tell you with a certainty born of experience that we always receive an answer, but that we sometimes fail to recognize it on account of preconceived notions about what that answer should be or how it should appear. The more open and nonjudgmental you can be, the more success you will experience. Remember that every creature, no matter how big or small, ugly or beautiful, soothing or frightening, is special and has a unique and powerful message to share with you.

Meditation Method

Find a comfortable place in which you can be alone and uninterrupted. You can play music if you choose, but I find that it is best to minimize distractions, and so be sure to silence your cell phone or put it in another place altogether while you do this. You will also want to have a notebook and pen nearby in which to record what you experience. Close your eyes, breathe comfortably, and repeat the following mantra (or a version of it that feels more comfortable to you) in your mind: "I am open to the totem [or spirit guide] that can help me the most at this time." Keep breathing, keep repeating the mantra to yourself, and it is likely that after a little while, you will begin to relax and drift off. This is the place where we go when we meditate or when we are "spacing out," and it is one of the best states in which to receive guidance. If you find yourself engaged in active thought again (wondering which guide will appear, for example), simply return to your mantra and your breath.

While you are here, you may see an animal or an insect, you may hear it announced by name, or you may hear one of the sounds it makes. You may be told to find a certain book or poem or movie, to go to a particular location, or to contact someone specific. You may also see or speak with someone dressed as a certain creature, in which case it is always best to treat these beings with the utmost respect, being sure to thank them for making their presence known to you, as well as for any guidance they share. However they are dressed is representative of your totem or spirit guide.

It is important not to judge the "quality" or intensity of what you experience while in a meditative state, as these things have absolutely no bearing whatsoever on the importance of the messages you receive. Whether your experience was as crisp and clear as though it were occurring in real life, whether it felt like a dream, or whether you simply heard sounds or saw images unfold in your mind's eye as you would when using your imagination, these are all perfectly valid experiences. And even if you fear that what came to you was simply a product of fantasy, it's still advisable to treat the episode as significant. If your mind selected that particular creature, there is a good reason, and exploring what it might mean for you may just yield the illumination you've been seeking.

When you come back to yourself, record what you saw, heard, and experienced during this time in your notebook. If your totem or spirit guide was shown or otherwise identified to you, then you can now go about getting to know it on a deeper level. Otherwise, follow the guidance you were given, and observe what happens. There have been numerous cases in my own life in which I heard the name of a person and knew I was supposed to call them, and during the course of the following conversation, that person brought up an encounter with a certain animal or insect. In other cases, I heard the title of a particular book, and even if it was a book whose subject matter had nothing whatsoever to do with spirituality, totems, or even animals, I would inevitably find within it a reference to the creature whose wisdom I required.

This exercise may feel odd or even frustrating at first, or you may have difficulty letting go and just being open. You can either continue trying, as practice really does make perfect here, or you can try one of the other methods in this chapter. None is better than the others. If it works and feels good, it's right for you.

Direct Askance Method

Purchase a book that contains information about a large assortment of birds and animals (or go to your local library or bookstore and take one off the shelf). Ask your guides to give you a page number to visit to help you connect with your totem or spirit guide. Go to the FIRST page number that pops into your head. No second-guessing yourself! Notice where your eyes are drawn first, and make a note about the animal mentioned in that section. If there is no animal mentioned, make note of what is contained in the section anyway, as you may have received important guidance on another matter. You can do this a few times, but I have found that the first or second answer is almost always the correct one.

Thank your guides, then ask that over the course of the next few days, they provide you with additional information about the totem or spirit guide whose wisdom would serve you best at this time. Take note of all animal or insect encounters you experience, and look for a pattern. If the same creature shows up at least three times (or if one of the appearances is especially intense), go with that one.

You can, if you choose, simply skip the first step and tell your guides that you would like to connect with the totem or spirit guide that will be of the most benefit to you at this time, then pay attention to what shows up in your experience, not forgetting that Beetle has as much to share as Lion. The book-exercise tends to be helpful to those who are new to this process, but it is not necessary. Remember, you don't need to engage in an elaborate process to access your intuition or to receive guidance from the Universe—your intuition is already there, ready and available, and the same is true of the Universe. You have only to ask It to help you.

Dream Method

Place a notebook and pen beside your bed before you go to sleep, and ask your guides to send you a dream to show you which totem or spirit guide would be of the most benefit to you at this time. Don't worry about whether or not you are usually someone who remembers their dreams. Intention is a *very* powerful thing, and you have just told the Universe that you intend to receive wisdom through dreams. This changes everything! Repeat this intention every night for at least a week, then record as many animal-related details as you can recall from your dreams, no matter how trivial or silly-seeming. Make sure you do it the *second* you wake up, as even if the dream was very vivid, you may forget it otherwise. Chances are, you will dream about your totem or guide at least once during the week.

On another note, dream interpretation is one of my favorite methods for helping my clients learn how to develop their intuition and employ it for their benefit. Once you start paying attention to your dreams and become comfortable interpreting their symbolism, you may be surprised by how much they enrich your understanding of your current situation. Dreams are so powerful, in fact, that I rely on their guidance to help me make many of the major decisions in my life, and this method has always served me well. For more information about dreams, see Chapter Ten.

JORDANA VAN

5 IF IT LOOKS LIKE A DUCK . . .

"Always behave like a duck—keep calm and unruffled on the surface, but paddle like the devil underneath."
—*Jacob M. Braude*

Some days, my life feels like a revolving door of animal-related experiences, with new creatures coming and going so quickly that I've long since given up keeping track of them. Unless you want to spend every waking moment—and I do mean *every* waking moment—frantically journaling about each instance in the hope of keeping a record of "proof," at a certain point, you just have to relax and accept that the necessity of proof has long passed. This is your life now. It's filled with strange and beautiful magic. And that magic often wears fur or feathers or scales.

When I first began writing this book series, I had not quite reached the point at which all of this was "normal", and the experiences that really stuck with me were the more dramatic ones, such as the episode I related in the first edition of this book in which Tiger appeared in my office.

Though what I experienced was the energy of a client's Tiger totem and not a living tiger, its presence was so overwhelmingly *visceral* that I could feel its breath on my ear and hear its growls as though it were sitting beside me. This was by far the most striking way in which I had received guidance at the time, and because it was such a powerful experience, it seemed the most appropriate to share. Too, if none of my readers could actually relate, I figured that at least the account would intrigue and amuse.

But after several years of doing this work—of interpreting animal experiences as a large part of the way in which I make my living—I have discovered that while the dramatic experiences can be more fun, and if you are a storyteller like me, provide fuel for entertainment *and* enlightenment, their only legitimate value when compared to the less "sparkly" experiences is that we tend to equate *bigger* with *better*, *truer*, and *more important*. And the bigger experiences are certainly easier for our logic-hungry minds to accept! If you are suddenly encountering bear-related paraphernalia everywhere, and then while you are camping, a grizzly bear shoves its way into your tent and snuggles up next to you for a cuddle, even the most skeptical brain is going to be forced to wonder if something significant has just occurred. On the other hand, if your home is suddenly invaded with ants, and ants appear in your desk at the office, and when you bite into your sandwich at lunch, you discover you've just eaten an ant, you're more likely to chalk it up to a seasonal issue triggering an ant infestation than an episode of personalized guidance from the Universe. And yet, it is these smaller, Ant-style experiences that make up the bulk of the guidance that most people receive. It might not seem like it at the time, but if we are willing to allow for the possibility that even the smallest occurrences may represent the hand of a loving Universe ushering us in the direction of our highest possible good, and that even the most insignificant-seeming facets of these experiences can have a special meaning, these messages can be every bit as earth-shattering as those that arrive with fireworks and fanfare.

I know this first-hand. I also apparently require reminding.

It was the beginning of spring when I developed a sudden obsession with feeding the ducks at one of our local ponds. There was no explanation—I just really wanted to feed the ducks! I even purchased a bag of bread from the grocery store and waited week after week for the weather to change, obsessively checking the temperature and precipitation forecast each morning and grumbling when it was better suited to ice-fishing than duck-feeding. I currently reside in the Midwestern United States, and while spring may have sprung, 50° F days with 40 ° F wind-chill were still the rule of the day, as were oppressive gray skies and sudden, soggy downpours. I did take a few optimistic trips to the pond with the bag of bread stuffed in my purse, but the wind was gusting to such a degree that I knew that any fragments I attempted to throw were likely to be blown right back into my face. And so the bread molded and had to be thrown away before it could be used as duck food.

In the mean time, I had ducks on the brain. I'd wake up in the middle of the night with a very particular image of a fluffy yellow duck in my mind's eye—not a duckling nor an adult, but a gangly juvenile. In the morning, when the alarm went off, it would be the first thing to pop into my head. My Facebook feed inexplicably became an unending parade of duck videos, and when my husband and I would turn on a cooking show, the chefs would be preparing some version of duck. There wasn't a doubt in my mind that this was a message, but I couldn't figure out why the Universe was sending it to me. I'd already *gotten* the message, thank you very much, and all this continued Duck-nonsense was beginning to feel a little redundant.

Duck often represents treading our emotional waters—appearing completely serene on top, but "paddl[ing] like the devil underneath." In other words, Duck can mean that while we may be dealing with a lot of emotional upheaval, we keep ourselves together and act like we're okay. At least, that's how I had always interpreted Duck's appearance in my life before. I'd long been familiar with Braude's famous quote, and so when Duck had previously appeared in my life, it was often a message to just suck it up and deal gracefully with whatever was occurring for me. "Quit whining, and keep paddling, Jordana," I'd often told myself.

But at this point, I'd already given myself that message. Repeatedly. Hell, yes, I was paddling like the devil! A week before, I had made a commitment to myself to finally let go of some huge, long-term areas of resistance in my life, which meant that I was really, truly going to let myself **FEEL** every emotion around these issues, rather than continue to do what I had been doing and continually acknowledge that the emotions were there while refusing to deal with them. This decision caused such an immediate, overwhelming upwelling of pain and fear and guilt that my first response was abject terror. So I felt that, too, and with it, the ego's frantic insistence that this was a *very* bad idea. Morning, noon, and night I was *feeling, feeling, feeling* . . . and it just didn't seem to stop! One emotion would finally subside, a moment of peace would flicker, and then another urgent emotion would arise, one after the other after the other. And so one minute I would rage, and the next I would cry, and the next after that I would be paralyzed with fear. It was a nightmare, and yet I knew that this was the only way I was going to get free of these chains once and for all.

And in the mean time, I had a job. I had clients who were paying me to be at the top of my intuitive and interpretive game, who needed me to be calm and centered enough to talk to their bodies and determine what they needed to heal. While working, I felt *very* much like Broad's duck—inside, I was *feeling* like mad, constantly applying the brakes on my reflexive tendency to repress while at the same time trying to corral the unending surge of thoughts that tried to change or extinguish the emotion. It was the mental equivalent of herding cats, if the cats were all high on catnip and also completely deranged. But on the outside, I was all business. I sounded calm and collected. I did the interpretations. I detached from my inner drama sufficiently to feel what was occurring in my clients, and to provide appropriate guidance. I received more positive feedback than ever before, and every new client seemed to want to provide a testimonial to encourage others to work with me. "Just keep acting like a duck, Jordana," I told myself, "and everything will be fine."

Fine? Despite all my encouraging self-talk, I felt anything but. One day, I would arrive at the blissful

Knowing that everything was okay, that it was safe to let go and relax and trust, and the next, I'd be right back to unmitigated terror and wondering where the hell that sense of security had gone. I knew that this was the experience of others who had gone through this process, and I knew that this process was the path to relief and healing, because I'd been doing it in smaller, less-intense doses for over a year with incredible results. But I wasn't sure I could keep it up at this level. I was scared, and in pain, and increasingly losing the faith that I'd ever get to the end of this insanity. I wanted to quit, and I spent a lot of time begging God for a sign that I was doing the right thing.

Yet there was only Duck, Duck, and more Duck. It was infuriating. Though while the ducks that appeared in my social media feeds, and in commercials, television shows, and random photographs were all adults, the one inside my head remained a fluffy, yellow juvenile. I'd taken notice of this, but the Universe had never sent me an animal of a particular *age* before, and I was in such bad shape, it only occasionally crossed my mind that it could be relevant. The closest I came to acknowledging that this might be significant was to question whether or not there really were yellow ducks. Had I ever actually seen a live one? Or was that just the color that artists and animators picked because it was "cute?" I remembered seeing animal cartoons and greeting cards featuring fluffy yellow ducklings, though all the ducklings I could ever recall seeing in the real world had been brown with hints of yellow. What about the classic rubber ducky? It was yellow, but was that based on something real, or just the toymaker's random choice? What color would a yellow duckling become when it grew up? Certainly not yellow. I was certain I'd never seen an adult duck of that hue. White? Did white ducks start as yellow ducklings? Donald Duck was white, but so were his nephews, Huey, Dewey, and Louie, and weren't they juveniles? If yellow ducklings became white ducks, shouldn't the nephews have been yellow?

Ah, the joys of over-thinking.

I could have Googled the answer, of course. But I didn't *want* to. I was unhappy, and I was hurting, and I felt terribly abandoned, because couldn't the Universe see how much I was suffering? Where was my guidance? Why keep telling me to just keep acting like a duck, when I was *doing* that? The Universe often sends spirit guides to help us better understand our situation, but I was certain I knew my situation, and it wasn't getting any better for being continuously thrust in my face! And so, even though I could have researched the age-aspect of my messenger, I refused to do so. It felt like a small act of rebellion against the Universe for giving me such a stupid, unhelpful message. It's funny how in seeking to punish someone else, we more often than not wind up punishing ourselves.

While my sanity felt like it was beginning to unravel, there was one part of me that was still operating perfectly, and that was my awareness that when Higher Self speaks, it's in our best interests to listen! So when the next duck video appeared on my Facebook news feed and I instantly knew I needed to share it, I didn't hesitate. I immediately posted it on my business page and admitted that while Duck was clearly my current spirit guide, I didn't yet know exactly what it was trying to tell me. The second the video had appeared, a part of me had thrown up the white flag and surrendered to the fact that if Duck was still there, I was missing something. I don't know why it is that sometimes surrender happens automatically, and sometimes we must consciously make the choice, but the timing always seems to be perfect. A bare handful of minutes after posting the video, a comment appeared from one of my more frequent readers, an upbeat guy with the sort of down-to-earth spirituality I'd always appreciated, and with whom I'd always enjoyed speaking. He suggested I ask the Duck how old it was.

My jaw hit the floor. I hadn't shared that the Duck appearing to me personally was of a particular age because I hadn't thought it sufficiently relevant to mention, and no one had *ever* suggested that I ask that question of a spirit guide.

Oh, God.

The significance of my Duck's age hit me at last. My stomach fluttered. My breath stopped. I felt my entire system *shift*, as parts of myself that I hadn't been aware were misaligned slid back into their proper place, and a wave of energy rolled from my spine to the crown of my head and back down again.

Sobs boiled out of my chest, and I burst into tears. Here I'd been in agony, railing at a Universe that I'd been convinced was ignoring me, and it had been trying to tell me that it *loved me* all along. It *had* been guiding me, but the message had been so simple, and so obvious, that I'd overlooked it.

What is a juvenile but an adult in training? I wasn't being told to "act like a duck"; rather, the Universe was telling me that I was learning how to *be* a duck. After all, despite Broad's quote making it sound as though a duck's internal life must be one of constant effort and anxiety, ducks are *born* to paddle through the water with ease. It is second-nature to them, just another part of being a creature that spends most of its life in and on the water. I was not being told to handle my internal craziness by gritting my teeth and pretending I was okay—I was being told that I was feeling especially crazy because I was still learning how to feel my emotions as they arose and let them go just as quickly. I was learning how to move through my internal waters as effortlessly as a duck moves through his pond, and more, that while I was no longer a "duckling" where this process was concerned, I still had a ways to go before I gained the mastery of a grown-up.

The Universe was telling me that I was on track, and that confusion and pain and mistakes were all part of the learning process, just as they are for any juvenile, human, duck, or otherwise. I was becoming a duck, but it wasn't going to happen overnight, so I needed to be patient with myself.

For the first time in weeks, I felt at peace. I was still massively uncomfortable, but I knew that this was to be expected, and that all was well, even if it didn't feel like it. I took a deep breath, let it out, and closed my eyes in gratitude. Then I returned to work and checked my email. The only new message was a newsletter from a wild animal park, and when I opened it, the first page featured a photograph of the fuzzy, yellow, juvenile duck they'd just rescued. This was the first time I'd seen an actual photograph of a juvenile, rather than an adult or duckling, and I took it as confirmation that I had indeed "gotten the message."

Duck continued to keep me company for another few months as I gained practice consistently feeling instead of trying to think my way through my emotions, change them, or pretend they weren't there. Never before had I encountered such a challenge to my concept of self-love, as to do this process successfully, I had to accept that I couldn't control the way I initially reacted to my experiences, and the perfectionist within me found this mightily difficult to swallow. I knew not to act on any negative emotions (and feeling does *not* mean acting), but I was positively aghast that these reactions occurred at all. For the first time in my life, I really understood what it meant to be human.

Some days were still difficult, but as time went on, the process did indeed become easier! Through the simple expedient of repetition, my feelings began to flow rather than being stopped and harassed at the gate. I learned how to recognize them when they were there and to just allow them to be what they were. I no longer had to give the feeling a name in order to allow it—I could simply be in the uncertainty of feeling and float there like a duck on a pond. And magically, little by little, the issues that had begun this madness began to dissolve. Here I had spent several years obsessively trying to think my way through them, and yet after a handful of months of simply feeling the emotions around them, they began to fragment and fall apart. As the emotional charge behind them was removed, they lost their meaning, and with it, the power they'd held over me.

Fears and desires and grievances that had felt absolutely overwhelming and immutable began to feel more like annoyances than Insurmountable Problems, and their presence in my awareness no longer dictated what kind of day I would have. Small Knowings appeared in my consciousness, a surety of the way that things were intended to be, regardless of the lack of logic to support them. I didn't need logic; I just Knew they were true, and so they were. Creativity surged; previously deflated by over-analyzing, now it was boundless, and expressed itself freely in a dozen different ways. Beauty was everywhere—even in ugliness. I'd denied myself emotional reactions to things that felt sad or lonely or painful or repulsive for so long that even disgust and sorrow had a pleasant edge. All emotions were valid, and so every part of myself was valid, and the disconnect between my mental self and my feeling self became less and less apparent.

I was becoming whole. Those few enormous issues I'd been refusing to Feel about had held far more sway over my life than I'd realized, and while Snake represented the overarching situation, and Great Snowy Owl had initially prodded me in the direction of exploring my feelings, the Universe was using Duck to keep me from chickening out when it got too hard! The better I learned to paddle gracefully through my emotional waters, the better my life flowed as a whole, and the more I became the person I truly *was*. And then one day, one of the biggest issues with which I'd been working simply ceased to matter. It hadn't changed, but *I* had. I could see how it didn't actually have the power over my life that I'd thought, and that I could be okay no matter what happened with it. It was inconsequential, irrelevant, an illusion. Unimportant.

The feeling of liberation this induced defies words.

On the same day this shift occurred, my husband and I decided to go to a farmer's supply store to which we had never been, despite passing it just about every day for years. I had the idea that they would have a decorative item I thought I wanted for my garden. Two seconds after we walked into the store, I heard peeping noises and dashed to the middle of the store where, in half a dozen different bins, there were piles and piles of fluffy, peeping baby chicks . . . and fluffy yellow ducks. Just out of the duckling stage, they were exactly what I had been seeing in my mind's eye these long months. I was riveted and couldn't stop staring and reflexively emitting "Squeee!" noises, much like a toddler at her first petting zoo. It was only through an act of sheer will that I obeyed the "Don't Touch!" sign and didn't reach into the bin to scoop one up to cuddle. If there hadn't been people browsing in the adjacent aisles, I might have done it anyway.

We didn't end up buying the item we'd come to find, but I didn't care. I knew I'd been sent there for the ducks, which was further proved when, on the way home, we turned into our subdivision and the large pond at its entrance featured something new—four adult ducks, two of them a crisp, snowy white. I'd never seen white ducks in the pond before, and I laughed, imagining those regal white ducks as awkward yellow flufflings like the ones I'd seen earlier.

Finally, it seemed, I was out of the awkward stage myself! It might be added that metaphysically, the color yellow is linked to the third chakra (solar plexus), where impulse-control is developed. We cannot choose how to handle our impulses if we do not understand what they actually are, and through feeling my emotions to such a degree, I was learning to understand the emotional responses that were actually driving me. This helped me determine what I actually *wanted* from each situation, and more, where I had the power to create what I wanted through action, and where I simply had to let the Universe take care of things for me. The color white is most often linked to the Divine, to surrendering to that holy, omnipotent force that knows where all the pieces of our personal puzzle belong and the most efficacious way to assemble them. By the time the white ducks appeared in the pond, surrendering to the Divine had become a regular part of my day. Trusting in this way still didn't come reflexively, but I engaged in the process frequently and fully enough that I could legitimately be called a "grown-up", rather like a young woman finally able to claim "adult" status because she had attained legal drinking age, but still a long, long ways from the wisdom and grace of an experienced elder. I still had a lot of learning to do, but the foundation had been laid.

Understanding Duck's message allowed me to see the building-process for what it really was, and I was able to recognize that the challenges with which I had been presented had been *exactly* what I'd needed. As much as I hated admitting it, pain had always been the only thing that would really stop me in my tracks and force me to make necessary changes; I'd been so afraid of things that felt good or easy that I couldn't trust them. Duck told me that I wasn't alone, that this wasn't for nothing, and that I would see the results in the way and time that were right for me. For now, this meant there might still be pain. In the future, there would be joy.

And so it was.

And so it is.

The Universe *wants* us to thrive. It wants us to live in trust and in wonder, and to be our whole selves unabashedly. It wants things to be easy for us, for the perfect answers to arrive in the perfect time, and for joy to be our natural way of being, rather than struggle or doubt. And it will send message after message after message in order to help us see this.

There is nothing we have to actively do to receive guidance—no years of study, no lengthy chanting or breathing, no spell, diet, drug, or ritual in which we must engage to be ready or worthy. Guidance is here now, all around us. All we have to do is allow ourselves to receive it.

Even now, the Universe is speaking to you.

Are you listening?

6 THE OWL PERSON AT A GLANCE

"A wise old owl lived in an oak.
The more he saw the less he spoke.
The less he spoke the more he heard.
Now why can't we all be like that bird?"
—Nursery rhyme, author unknown

Natural Strengths

- Sensitive to the moods of others

- Analytical

- Sensual

- Protective

- Creative

- Truth-seekers

- Clairaudient

- Excellent writers, researchers, historians, and craftsmen

- Potential to be superb healers and counselors

- Honest and direct

- Focused

- Independent

- Love to learn and explore

Qualities to Develop

- Feeling rather than simply analyzing their feelings

- Trusting their impressions of others

- Exploring themselves to the same degree they scrutinize others

- Heeding their intuitive signals *when they arise*

- Flexible thinking

- Releasing the need for justice or fairness when appropriate

- Recognizing when they are allowing details to overwhelm the larger picture

- Learning when to speak, and when to stay silent

- Humility

- Letting go of old wounds, limiting beliefs, and limiting attachments to old experiences

- Self-acceptance

JORDANA VAN

7 THE OWL PERSON'S JOURNEY

Ruled by the Moon, Lack Waterproof Feathers

Resulting traits*: Mood swings * Sensitivity to the feelings of others * Require considerable time alone * Tend to analyze emotions rather than* feel *them * Heightened feminine energy * Maternal protective tendencies * Creative*

Resulting lessons*: Trust intuition to tell you when to avoid certain people/places/events * Make sure to secure adequate rest and time alone * Learn to balance analyzing emotions with feeling them * Prioritize creative time*

Thought by many to be exclusively nocturnal hunters, many owls are actually active during the day, some even primarily so. This misconception has created a long-standing association between owls and darkness, as well as between owls and the moon, the latter of which rules our emotions. And while this association may be only partially accurate, its lengthy history means that those who resonate with Owl are more likely to be deeply feeling creatures prone not only to extreme mood swings, but to sensing the moods of others.

Having Owl as a totem is a great deal like having one's moon in a water sign (Pisces, Cancer, or Scorpio) in one's astrological chart. Individuals with this arrangement tend to be extremely sensitive to other people's hurt and pain and therefore to have issues with emotional boundaries; like psychic sponges, they unintentionally sop up and absorb others' emotional energy until they aren't quite sure where they end and others begin. This can lead to feelings of being overwhelmed, confused, depressed, exhausted, apathetic, or even out of control. It can also create feelings of loneliness and resentment, as the Owl Person feels like they have simply become a repository for everyone else's drama, without having anywhere to put their own!

This intense vulnerability to the emotions of others is further compounded by the owl's response to getting wet. Unlike other birds of prey, owls lack waterproof feathers, which makes flying in the rain difficult if not completely impossible. When conditions are stormy for a lengthy period, an owl is unable to hunt and therefore at serious risk of starvation. If it currently has chicks that are depending upon it for nourishment, they may starve as well. For Owl People, being exposed to the emotional "storms" of others can prevent them from taking care of themselves, as well as those people and things that are most important to them. All of that external emotion can literally "soak them to the bone", so much so that they lose contact with what *they* really need, and what *they* really feel. When this occurs, they are more likely to become ill, and to feel extremes of emotion that they do not understand (because the emotion isn't actually theirs to begin with!). And while it is possible even for Owl People to learn to avoid absorbing the emotions of others, their best defense is simply to "stay out of the rain!"

This being the case, it is vitally important that Owl People learn to pay attention to intuitive cues and honor their gut-feelings. These will tell them when they need to avoid going to a particular place or should steer clear of another person, no matter how safe or appealing the situation or person may externally appear. As they are so easily overwhelmed on a psychic level, it should not be surprising that it is normal for Owl People to require a great deal of time by themselves and to largely prefer occupations where their physical contact with others is minimal. During their me-time, they are able to rest, reconnect with their own needs, and if necessary, detoxify themselves of all the energetic garbage they have absorbed.

Despite feeling everything so very deeply, Owl People will rarely behave as drama queens or let their feelings run away with them. Their fierce hunger to understand and explore the greater mysteries of the universe extends to the realm of feeling as well, and so rather than give themselves the luxury of simply feeling, intense emotions are often pushed to the side for analysis. Owl People want to know if their emotions are *valid* before they allow themselves to have them, which can often incorrectly give others the impression that Owl People are cool or closed off.

This need to analyze first and feel later (and only after the feeling has been deemed appropriate to the situation) can also mean that Owl People come to the wrong conclusions about why they are feeling the way that they are! Many emotions simply cannot be understood by the mind alone, as the mind's analytical nature will seek to impose the best-fitting logical explanation onto the emotion rather than allowing the emotion to speak for itself. For example, an Owl Person may find themselves feeling unreasonably angry with their spouse when s/he comes home in the evenings. Because their spouse has been coming home late and is therefore missing their old routine of sharing dinner together, the Owl Person decides that this must be the reason they are feeling angry, even though they know that this is a consequence of their spouse's new work-schedule, and so it is to be expected. And so they tell themselves they simply shouldn't be angry with their spouse, then are surprised when the anger continues or perhaps grows even stronger! Had they let themselves feel the emotion in its entirety when it occurred rather than rushing to analytical judgment, they would have discovered that they were not angry about their spouse's late return, nor with the change in their dinner routine, nor even with their spouse at all; rather, they were angry because the multitude of chores that the spouse used to do was now falling to them, because the spouse had less time to do them. What they were *really* angry about then, was the imbalance in household tasks and the sense of unfairness that this was creating. Further feeling would have lead to the conclusion that many of these chores were not even tasks that needed doing so often, but the Owl Person had been sticking to the old schedule simply because it was the original way of doing things. At this point, the anger could be set aside and balance could be returned to the situation by first determining which chores had to be done with such regular frequency and which did not, and second, by looking at ways to recreate a sense of fairness. Perhaps the Owl Person, now aware of what they were actually feeling, might decide that they actually *want* to do some of those additional chores, because it feels good to them to relieve some of their spouse's burden. Perhaps their spouse could do some of the chores in the morning before s/he leaves for work, or on a weekend. Or, if neither party is able to feel good about doing the chores originally done by the spouse, the option of hiring a housekeeper could also be explored!

Owl people excel in determining what makes others tick, but can have a difficult time doing it for themselves, largely because they just have so many *feelings* about everything! Just as the moon moves relentlessly through her phases each month, so, too, do Owl People tend to move through extremes of emotion. Something may hardly be noteworthy one day, then feel like a huge deal the next, and this roller-coaster of feeling can be absolutely exhausting. With practice *feeling in the moment* instead of automatically analyzing, Owl People can greatly increase their ability to flow with their feelings rather than feel buffeted by them. Emotions that are repressed, which is often what occurs when analysis is employed in *place* of feeling, do not simply disappear; they continue to control our day-to-day operations from the realm of the subconscious mind. Emotions that are *felt* are eventually released (which is why venting can feel so very good and makes us feel so much lighter afterwards, even when the circumstances that prompted the venting have not changed)[3]. When an Owl

Person notices that an emotion that they thought they understood is refusing to abate, it's a good idea to assume that they missed something, and rather than trying to think the answers into being, to try to get themselves to *feel* them. This does not mean that they should not think about their feelings at all, only that they should not think to the *exclusion* of feeling. A helpful way to know whether or not they are getting closer to arriving at a correct interpretation of their emotion's meaning is to remember that purely logical conclusions may make *sense*, but *correct* conclusions tend to feel like an "Ah-ha!" moment or an enormous sense of relief.

In addition to its impact upon an Owl Person's emotions, the moon has long been a symbol of femininity, sensuality, and motherhood. Owl Women[4] tend to radiate mystery and sexuality, to enjoy the thrill of romance and delight in being chased; nevertheless, they are neither soft nor likely to tolerate someone's attempts to dominate them.

---

[3] For more information on emotional wellbeing, I highly recommend Dr. David R. Hawkins' excellent text *Letting Go: The Pathway of Surrender* (Hay House, 2014), which describes in detail the mental and physical effect of repressed emotions versus the liberation of feeling.

[4] For the sake of simplicity, I have chosen to use "Women" to indicate those who identify as female and "Men" to refer to those whose identify as male. This is for the sake of clarity only, and not to imply that to be a man means that one must also be male, nor that to be a woman means one must be female. If you identify as a male, then the information pertaining to Owl Men is intended for you, and if you identify as a female, then please refer to the information about Owl Women.

They are also especially intolerant of threats to those in their care; Owl Women are devoted mothers and aggressive defenders of their children. These are not smother-mothers—they know when it is time for their child to leave the nest, even if they must push the little birdie out themselves!—but they can generally be counted on to be there when their children need them. Owl Men also tend to be especially protective parents, and to be more aware of the feminine portions of their being. They are likely to have a stronger connection with their emotional selves then most other men, to be more romantic, and to be more nurturing, likely being unusually good listeners and counselors. At the same time, however, while these men might initially be mistaken as "soft", they are no more so then their female counterparts. These men know what they want and will not tolerate a relationship in which they are made to feel inferior.

The moon is also linked to our creative expression, and Owl People require a creative outlet with roughly the same urgency as they require food and water. Without regular engagement in some form of creativity—even something as simple as doodling on a scrap of paper while they are on hold with their internet provider—Owl People tend to become apathetic and listless. Creativity also acts as an anchor for these largely mental beings, as it allows them to take internal processes and externalize them, providing physical proof of their existence; this prevents them from drifting off into dreams and becoming completely detached from their realty. Expressing themselves creatively is a vital act of grounding, and it is therefore imperative that the Owl Person make time to be creative as often as necessary.

Targeted Hearing

Resulting traits: *Truth-seekers * Human lie-detectors * Especially intolerant of injustice and unfairness * Clairaudient*

Resulting lessons: *Applying the same degree of questioning to themselves as to others * Trusting their intuition * Learning that it is sometimes necessary to surrender the need to see truth revealed * Heeding songs/sounds/words and other auditory cues that appear with particular frequency or in pronounced fashion*

Owls may be most notable for their striking, lambent eyes, but while their vision is very good, it is their hearing that is their most exceptional feature. In general, an owl's auditory range is comparable to that of a human; what sets it apart is the heightened sensitivity to sounds in the highest frequencies, specifically the sort of high-pitched squeaks made by their favorite prey. Sound-channeling facial discs coupled with asymmetrical ear openings (in nocturnal owls) also work together to allow the owl to determine its' prey's exact location in complete darkness, in high grasses, or beneath bushes, leaves, or even snow.

Owls possess a much more complicated medulla than that of others birds. This is the area of the brain that is associated with hearing, and its sophistication—in the form of a much greater number of neurons and therefore neuronal connections—is what makes it possible for the owl to make moment-to-moment use of the information received by its ears. Many owls are able to discern the direction of their prey by gauging the minute difference in time between when a sound is perceived by their left ear versus when it is perceived by their right (a difference sometimes as small as 30 millionths of a second!); they then turn their head until the sound is received by both ears at once, at which time they know that their prey is right in front of them. Whether the prey is spatially higher or lower is also determined in this fashion, as the asymmetrical placement of their ear openings means that sound will hit either the higher ear or lower ear first, at which point the time difference can be compared and a location calculated. These comparisons and facial adjustments happen so quickly that it is possible for the owl to change course mid-flight if the prey happens to move. An owl's hearing is further enhanced by a facial disk that acts like a satellite dish, catching and funneling sound to its ears and allowing the owl to hone in on its prey with even greater accuracy.

In Owl People, it is these adaptations that make them truth-hunters without equal. Owl People are primed to sense and spot all the little inconsistencies between the person one is attempting to present to the world—and the person that one actually *is*. It is generally a waste of time to lie to an Owl Person; just as in the case of the tiny squeaks made by their prey, Owl People have a unique ability to hear exactly what makes you feel the most vulnerable, the parts of yourself that you would rather conceal, whether these are lies that you are intentionally telling, lies by omission, subtle inconsistencies between word and deed, or secrets you would rather not speak. As rapidly as an owl can make mental calculations between auditory time differences, Owl People can weigh the physical evidence (which is processed by the right side of the body) against what their intuition is telling them (processed by the left side of the body) and conclude that something in what you are saying (or not saying) is awry. They may not know exactly *what* that is, but they will know that there *is* something being concealed or corrupted, and they will usually have a pretty strong suspicion of its nature.

And Owl People, once they are aware that you are somehow vulnerable, have a very tough time letting it go. In an owl, locating a vulnerable creature would mean the creature would be rapidly caught and eaten. It is prey, and this is the proper use of prey. In an Owl Person, knowing that you are hiding something but are refusing to fess up about it drives them crazy. That truth that you are hiding is their prey, and you are preventing them from having it! Owl People simply *cannot* tolerate an inconsistency between what they intuitively feel about someone and how a person appears to others; they will obsess endlessly about the contrast, often to the exclusion of all else in their life. And this means asking questions—lots and lots of questions! An owl's auditory targeting ability requires that its prey continue to make noise; were it to stop, the owl would suddenly be rendered "blind", and the prey would be more likely to escape. In Owl People, trying to figure out exactly what their intuition is telling them often means making a whole lot of "noise", questioning the issue relentlessly to get closer and closer to the truth until they have either exhausted all possible questions, or until truth has been revealed.

It is interesting to note that Owl People, who can spot falsehood, denial, and weakness in others so readily, often have a difficult time perceiving it in themselves. In most cases, part of becoming a mature Owl Person involves learning to apply the same forthright questioning to themselves as they apply to others. "What is causing me to act this way?" "How do I *really* feel about my circumstances?" "What situation in my life am I refusing to acknowledge, because I am afraid to do so?" "What do I believe about my relative degree of power in this situation? Do I feel like a victim?" These and other probing queries are what will allow the Owl Person to attain access to their *personal* truth in the same way that they are able to discern truth in others.

Much like those born under the sign of Libra, Owl People hunger for both balance and justice. They want word and deed to align perfectly, and when it does not, they feel out of sorts. This is particularly true when they feel like someone is getting away with something; they perceive this as unfair, and it makes them angry! They believe that the only way to feel better again is to bring truth and appearance back into harmony, which means either picking over the problem until they determine that *they* are wrong (which is not usually the case, even if the Owl Person convinces themselves that it is), until they figure out exactly what is being concealed and have unearthed the evidence to prove it, or until the other party confesses.

In some cases, it can be an awfully long wait, and the longer the truth remains concealed, the more likely the Owl Person will be to conclude that they must be wrong. Because they are such incredibly intuitive *feelers* but also such profound *thinkers*, it is not difficult for them to poke holes in an intuitive hunch, and they will often second-, third-, and fourth-guess themselves into utter confusion. This may mean that they place their trust in the wrong people, unable to believe that the person might be bad for them, because even though their intuition is shouting at them, the physical evidence to the contrary is so strong. It may also be that the Owl Person allows others to make them feel badly for harboring suspicions. Other times, the Owl Person themselves invalidates their intuitive hunches because they've not yet made peace with their uniqueness and want to seem "normal"; while their intuition is clearly speaking to them, they are discomfited by the belief that others will judge them for relying upon it, and so they do what is "logical" in order to fit it or keep from making waves. Whatever the case, it is almost always part of an Owl Person's journey to not only develop faith in their intuition, but to learn to abide by its messages as much as possible.

Often, this will mean acting in a way that is in complete opposition to what logic would dictate, refusing to place one's trust in someone with excellent character-references, for example, or ignoring "expert" advice about how one ought to proceed in certain circumstances. In other cases, this will mean that they must simply accept that while *they* know the truth about someone or something, it is beyond their power to do anything about it (or more often, it is not their *place* to do anything about it), and so they must stop obsessing about it and simply let karma do its job. Nothing is occurring save they are ruining their own sense of peace, and so letting go is an act of love for themselves, not an approval of the injustice of which they are aware.

An Owl's heightened hearing abilities also produce another effect in those for whom Owl is a totem: clairaudience. In clairaudient individuals, auditory phenomena such as music, words, and all form of sounds from traffic noise to television commercials to birdsong are more likely to act as messages from their Higher Selves. These sounds may actually be occurring in real time, they may be spontaneously remembered, or they may simply be imagined, such as cases in which we hear a sound that others do not, or we believe we have heard someone calling our name. I am especially clairaudient, and almost every time that the latter has occurred for me, if I am able to determine whose voice I am hearing, it turns out that the person *was* indeed wanting to speak with me, and usually for an important reason! Similarly, the name of a book or movie may suddenly shout itself in one's mind, with these items possessing some wisdom related to one's current circumstances, or one may imagine the sound of an animal whose guidance is particularly significant at this time (such as imagining coyotes howling or hearing a lion's roar).

Songs are another common way in which people experience clairaudience. I will often awake in the morning with a particular song lyric ping-ponging between my ears, and when I turn on the radio, this song will be playing. The lyrics typically relate to something that happens later in the day, or they act as a message from my guides about something to which I need to be paying more attention, some action I need to take, or something I need to be doing differently. Sometimes the words of the song *are* the answer, such as in a more recent case in which I asked the Universe to let me know if a situation with which I was dealing was almost over. The next morning, I woke with Mikky Ekko's song, "Smile", playing between my ears, whose chorus begins "Smile, the worst is yet to come." You can imagine how I felt about that one! And while yes, the worst *was* yet to come, when it arrived, I felt much calmer having received a prior heads-up, and I was able to move through it quickly, serenely (mostly), and without lasting harm.

Fixed Gazes and Flexible Necks

*Resulting traits: Focused * May not notice problems until it is too late * Able to quickly shift between interests * Jacks- and Janes-of-all-trades * Creative thinkers and problem-solvers*

*Resulting lessons: Acting upon intuitive cues when they appear * Applying the same degree of analysis to their own feelings and behaviors as they do to others * Becoming aware of their own limiting beliefs and/or judgmental thinking*

The eyes of an owl are impressively sized, occupying over fifty percent of the space in their skulls. While the large size and ability to expand their pupils beyond the range of a human's allows them to see well in low light, the tubular shape of the eye means that they cannot roll or shift them like others animals. Owl eyes stare straight ahead, immobile in their sockets, and so Owl People have a rare gift for being able to focus on a task or concept for long periods of time without becoming distracted. When they want something, it is difficult for them to think of anything else, and they will invest themselves completely in its pursuit. As truth-seekers first and foremost, this makes Owl People excellent researchers and historians, able to pour over complicated texts in search of revelation for hours on end. It also makes them superior craftsmen, their ability to concentrate for such long stretches giving them a tolerance for nuance and detail work that would otherwise bore or frustrate others.

Nevertheless, here again we find the tendency of Owl people to become so fixated on something that their attention can border on obsession. Just like the owl that is so involved in pursuing its prey as it scurries across the highway that it is utterly unaware of the oncoming car, Owl People can become so caught up in whatever they are doing that they completely ignore what is occurring around them, even blatant warning signals heralding oncoming danger. Owls do not have good peripheral vision—to see something to either side of them, they must turn their head—and so when they are *especially* focused on something, it is often only the most intense distractions (and sometimes seemingly out-of-the-blue traumas) that are able to force them to shift their "gaze" to see what is going on around them. This can be a brutal shock to the Owl Person's system; here they were busily invested in their latest project and thought everything was fine, and then, *bam!* Life takes a sudden turn, or they are slammed with a loss, and the Owl Person feels like they've been hit by a truck.

Given the tendency of the Owl Person to overlook the flaws in their reality until it crumbles around them, how then are they to remain safe and happy? Are they destined to be endlessly blindsided? After several years of working with Owl People, I have observed that Owl People are not *blind* to these signals—rather, the signals are simply not taken seriously when they arise. The Owl Person may write the signal off because they do not trust themselves and think the signal must therefore be nonsense, they may ignore it because the signal is uncomfortable (and then forget about it entirely once they re-immerse themselves in their work), or they were supremely excited about doing whatever they were doing at the time the signal arrived, and the signal is less interesting than the task at hand! An Owl Person hungrily devouring a new text on his favorite topic is going to find the subtle intuitive tingling warning him that something is amiss in his marriage far less interesting—and far less enjoyable!—than that text! And so rather than investigate the signal, he simply buries himself in his work once more. It is not until those intuitive tingles become screeching alarms (perhaps in the form of his wife packing her suitcase and leaving, at which point, the marriage may be beyond salvage) that the Owl Person looks around and wonders what on earth is going on. Additionally, Owl People who *do* become aware of these signals may turn them into yet another obsession, picking them apart until the intuitive piece is completely lost, ending up in a tangle of mixed feelings and hearsay, at which point, they feel utterly paralyzed and again seek solace in their work, leaving the problem precisely as it was before.

Owls have excellent long vision, but close-up their eyesight is poor. It is always going to be easier for the Owl Person to analyze others than it is to analyze themselves (especially since an owl's vision is also extremely sensitive to movement, so when someone else does something interesting, Owl People tend to immediately lose interest in exploring themselves and seize on whatever is occurring with the other person), and so it is inevitable that a certain degree of self-discipline will be necessary in order for the Owl Person to remain sufficiently aware of both critical internal forces and the reality that those forces are creating. Owl People must learn that intuitive signals are *not* to be ignored, and that while logic does indeed have its place—as well as the relentless questioning for which they are famous—the *truth* can be found not in the mind, but in that ephemeral sensation of "rightness" and Knowing without knowing how one Knows. When intuition says something is wrong, the Owl Person needs to pay attention and act accordingly.

Nature has compensated for the owl's fixed stare by providing it with additional vertebrae and enhanced muscles that create a uniquely flexible neck. Owls cannot rotate their heads in a full circle as many believe, but most species can twist them at least 180 degrees to look straight behind them (with the great horned owl able to turn its head 270 degrees, a full three-quarters of the way!). Moreover, an owl's bones and blood-vessels are adapted to allow them to turn their heads from side to side at a speed that would literally give other creatures a stroke. This produces a fascinating ability in Owl People, namely, the capacity to shift almost instantly from being utterly fixated on one thing to being just as fixated on something else. *Everything* that snags an Owl Person's attention is given the totality of their energy and passion. The topic may occupy them for a year, or it may occupy them for five minutes, but for the duration of the Owl Persons' interest, it will be investigated and pursued with singular vigor. This has the effect of making Owl People consummate Jacks- and Janes-of-all-trades, and master of more than a few! With so much intensity poured into their pursuit of a skill or idea or project, and with such an enormous capacity for focused study, it is no wonder that they do so many things well.

Additionally, the owl's ability to turn its head to such a

degree is directly linked to the Owl Person's ability to be flexible in their thoughts. A stiff or inflexible neck is often evidence in humans of inflexible thinking, and healing the issue most often involves asking the person to identify the ways in which they are perceiving situations in their life in a limited or black-and-white fashion. Therefore, part of an Owl Person's development often involves learning to develop flexibility of thought. This is more than being open-minded; it is becoming adept at spotting the ways in which they may be inappropriately judging themselves, others, and situations, with particular emphasis on any limiting beliefs they are holding about themselves and their lives. Again, Owl People are excellent at honing in on the truth of what is occurring in others, but they may completely ignore an internal belief that is holding them back from being completely happy. "What do I believe about myself and my role in this situation?" is always an excellent question for them to ask themselves when they find themselves stuck or unfulfilled, as well as "Are there any other angles from which I could examine this situation?" "How could I look at it differently?" "How could I be flexible here?" At this point, Owl People often discover that the reason they are stuck is because they believe that the way forward has to *look a certain way*, and they are not allowing the Universe to work its magic and provide an unexpected exit-strategy. When Owl People (and the rest of us!) release their preconceived notions, problems often miraculously solve themselves.

This capacity for flexible thinking also makes mature Owl People supremely creative thinkers. They are able to examine every aspect of a situation—to look at it from all angles—and pick it apart until a solution presents itself. If you're stranded on a desert island, an Owl Person would definitely increase your odds for survival.

Beaks that Cut, Crush, and Tear

Resulting traits*: Blunt * Forthright * Honest * Friends must have a great deal of confidence*
Resulting lessons*: Giving one's opinions only when asked*

All owls have short, curved, downward-facing beaks that terminate in a hook and overlap in a scissor-like fashion, enabling the owl to cut and tear its prey to pieces. The beak also possesses significant crushing-power, which it uses when its feet and talons are not sufficient to kill the prey mid-flight. Metaphysically, the features of an animal's mouth are linked to the way in which we express ourselves via speech. Are we the sort of person who is always soft-spoken, diplomatic, politically correct, and desperately does not want to hurt anyone's feelings? Do we tell long, detailed, meandering stories? Or, are we the sort of person who—while not actually *wanting* to hurt someone's feelings in most cases—may often wind up doing so anyway because we are blunt, unapologetic speakers of the truth as we perceive it and also have little patience for unnecessary details? Owl People are the latter; they do not generally *want* to hurt people, but they believe that the truth is the truth, and that nothing useful comes from living in denial. They also do not want to hear your long-winded stories or excuses—they want you to get right to the point, and for the point to be something *significant*.

Unless you really want an honest answer, an Owl Person is not the one whose opinion you want to seek about your new hair-cut, nor the one you should ask if those jeans "make you look fat." To them, the emotional suffering you may experience at hearing the truth is secondary to the truth itself. Yes, it may hurt to know they think that your new hair cut makes you look like a hedgehog, but wouldn't you rather know this, thinks the Owl Person, than go out on the town believing you look fabulous when you do not? Owl People are particularly sensitive to your degree of pride in yourself; if they do not think it is appropriate, they will tell you, and so it is not wise to go fishing for compliments from an Owl Person. Not only will you not get the compliment, but they are likely to take you down another notch or three while they're at it. They are not being malicious; they simply feel that maintaining what they perceive as a false fantasy of deservedness is not doing you any good. Owl People can cut to pieces those with whom they find themselves in conversation, whether these are casual acquaintances or close friends and family members, just as an owl's beak can rend and tear its prey.

This being the case, it takes a particularly confident individual to survive a friendship with an Owl Person. Abrasive commentary notwithstanding, it usually becomes apparent pretty rapidly that the Owl Person has a bead on one's deepest, darkest secrets and sees immediately through one's lies (most especially the lies one tells oneself). Unless you are the kind of person who is so confident in yourself that you never feel the need to prevaricate, or who simply does not *have* any secrets, being around an Owl Person is really going to put you on edge!

Too, while Owl People are usually supremely loving individuals, the way in which they *show* their love—telling others truths about themselves that they often do not wish to hear—is often perceived as an act of insensitivity, or even outright maliciousness. The Owl Person will not let you get away with fooling yourself, even if doing so makes you feel better, partially because they cannot stand to see a truth concealed, and partially because they simply cannot understand why you *wouldn't* want to embrace the truth when living in denial is doing nothing but keeping you stuck.

If you are friends with an Owl Person, it is always best to keep in mind that when they are pointing out what they perceive as your flaws, they are often trying to help you. And they would *love* if you asked them for advice on how to do this! If you are an Owl Person, however, and have noticed that your friendships always seem strained, you would do well to ask yourself how often you give your opinion when it has not been requested. If someone asks a question and receives an honest answer that hurts them, the blame rests with them for asking. But when someone consistently points out someone else's flaws when they have not been asked to do so, that person is being exceptionally presumptuous! Remember that people only change when they are *ready* to change, and that no amount of forcing will create lasting results. Instead, we can only be the kind of loving person to whom someone will come when they are ready for assistance or advice, and we can make an effort to deliver even uncomfortable truths with compassion and gentleness. An Owl Person's friends will be aware that they are the sort of person who always tells it like it is, and so when they are *ready* for an Owl Person's take on their lives, they will ask. If you truly love your friends, trust them to know when it is time to face the music. Far more good will come of it, and your friendships will feel far more satisfying[5].

Talons that Crush, Pierce, and Rend

*Resulting traits: Capacity for humility and compassion * Can become so fixated on details they overlook the big picture*

*Resulting lessons: Determining when it is and is not appropriate to reveal the truth * Flexible thinking*

An owl's feet possess incredible crushing-power, with each foot's four toes terminating in a razor-sharp talon that is used to both grab their prey mid-flight and pierce the prey to kill it. When snagging their prey, an owl's feet are actually functioning like hands, and metaphysically, our hands are linked to reaching, grabbing, and holding what we

---

[5] It is important to note here that while most *friendships* benefit from waiting to speak the truth about someone until that person is ready to hear it, this is not true for all relationships. In a relationship in which two people literally depend upon each other—such as in a marriage—one party's refusal to face a difficult truth (when one spouse has a drinking problem, for example, or a gambling habit), may impact the other party's mental, physical, and financial wellness. In these cases, forcing the issue and telling the other person something that they do not want to hear may be a necessary part of bringing the relationship back into balance and protecting oneself. Unfortunately, there are no rules to tell you when to hold your tongue and when to speak up; rather, you must listen to your heart and trust that it will tell you when to speak and what to say.

want in life. Given the fierceness of the owl's talons, it is no wonder that those who resonate with Owl can sometimes "stab" or "eviscerate" others as part of achieving what they desire.

As previously discussed, Owl People have a hard time learning to trust themselves. Once they do, they will inevitably encounter a second lesson: determining whether or not it is appropriate to act on that information. When one can see and hear so much of what others are trying to hide, the hunger to be the one to expose the truth can be almost impossible to resist. After all, there is a great deal of personal satisfaction to be had in being the one who drags that skeleton out of someone's closet and parades it down the street! If one is an investigative journalist, or a detective or an attorney, this is not necessarily a bad thing, and "crushing" or "eviscerating" others may even be an essential fixture of one's career; it is not so commendable if one makes a habit of exposing the secrets of their friends and loved ones or pointing out their flaws, particularly if this is done primarily for the thrill of it. Many Owl People need to learn to set aside their egos long enough to consider how others will react to hearing the Owl Person's take on their behavior, or what certain revelations will do to a person's life. There are times when an Owl Person needs to remember to see people as *people*—as creatures of flaw and feeling—and not as programs or constructs. People have lives that will be affected when certain truths are exposed, and these lives contain spouses and parents and children who may be hurt in the fall-out. Some things are kept private for good reason. Too, there is a big difference between bringing a truth to light because it will do some legitimate good, or because it will bring an evil-doer to justice, and exposing a truth just because one *can*.

Owl People are capable of both tremendous humility and compassion, both of which arise from the understanding that truth-seeing has a purpose beyond wounding or controlling others, or as a bolster for the ego. In its purest form, the ability to perceive the truth in others is a priceless gift that can comfort, uplift, and help others grow. Not all Owl People will develop humility or compassion, just as not all Owl People become "wise." The concept of the owl as a "wise" bird is most often considered a western concept, a hold-over from the days when the Greek goddess of wisdom, Athena, chose a "little owl" for her companion, after which the Romans paired their own goddess of wisdom, Minerva, with an owl as well. In other cultures, owls have been alternately worshipped and feared, respected as protectors and condemned as reincarnations of the devil. In India, the great moon-eyes that some cultures view as shining with the light of knowledge are seen instead as vacant, and the owl is associated with the shyster, with sneaky business dealings and a deceitful nature. Knowing someone's secrets can be used to blackmail someone or heal them, to bring down a dictatorship or weaken a healthy democracy, and it is up to the Owl Person to choose what kind of person they will be. Not all Owl People will choose the same way.

Though an owl's feet are metaphysically comparable to hands, an additional metaphysical interpretation can be applied to the toes themselves. An owl's foot has four toes, three of which are usually facing forward when flying. When perching, however, or when clutching their prey, a uniquely flexible joint allows one toe to swivel to the rear, neatly encircling the prey with two toes on each side and making it less-likely the prey can wriggle free. Flexible toes are a crucial part of an owl's ability to nourish itself and therefore to enjoy a healthy life. In humans, our toes represent the details involved in our life's forward progress, i.e., the degree to which we feel the path ahead is clear and all the moving parts are working together to bring us to our goal. Healthy, flexible toes are a sign of an optimistic and flexible approach to one's future, while stiff, sore, stubbed, or broken toes are indicative of an unhealthy focus on perceived roadblocks. Flexibility always equals success, while limiting beliefs keep us stuck.

I cannot tell you how many clients I've talked with who, when they feel like their lives just aren't working out because certain details refuse to resolve themselves, seem to endlessly stub and/or break their toes! In particular, I recall two different clients who came to me after they were released from prison, and who each broke their big toes in the year following their release. Their criminal convictions felt like a MAJOR impediment to the lives they wanted to create for themselves, an awful, monstrous detail they were forced to confront day after day. Because of their criminal records, they said, they each felt like "losers" who would never have anything that they wanted.

Owl People can get awfully hung up on details. Often, they become convinced that these things are standing in the way of their happiness, yet ruminating on them simply keeps them right where they are. If they are going to move forward in their lives, they need to be more flexible, allowing themselves to feel their frustrations until they abate and space is opened in which they can listen calmly to their hearts, at which point, they will know which details are important and which are just noise. It may feel like *everything* in one's life is going wrong, but more often than not, only a handful of aspects are actually an issue. Once the Owl Person knows which aspects to examine and which to ignore, an intuitive approach (What *feels* the most important?) will help them focus their energies in the places where they will actually do some good.

In the case of my aforementioned clients, their criminal records at first felt like a barrier to every good thing that they wanted. They were angry about having to live with their parents, about not being able to find the kind of job they wanted, about not being able to afford a car, not being able to afford to date, and about constantly feeling badly about themselves. Each of these things felt like an enormous weight on their hearts and minds, and they were overwhelmed with depression. But when I asked them to calmly try to *feel* which of these circumstances was the biggest issue for them at the time, they both concluded that the way they perceived their criminal records as affecting their ability to get a job was the most significant. In fact, it was the lynch-pin; if they could get a good job, they could live on their own, buy a car, have enough money to date, eventually get married, and would feel a good deal better about themselves. All other details were then set aside, and having only one issue to consider, they now felt much calmer. A brief application of that famous Owl Person creative thinking was then employed, leading to one client coming up with a job that he could do that would not require much start-up capital, which interested him greatly, and for which he was well-qualified, while the other suddenly remembered an old friend who ran a company doing his preferred kind of work, and who might have a job opening. Things did not right themselves overnight, but obtaining a well-paying job they were proud to do wound up being the first step to healing the trauma of having been incarcerated and bringing good things back into their lives.

Silent Flight

Resulting traits: Capacity to be excellent listeners, teachers, counselors, and healers

Resulting lessons: Patience * Silence * Offering wisdom out of love, rather than the need to be right or to control

The feathers of an owl's wings are softer than those of other birds of prey, and those on the wings' leading edges feature fine serrations. Together, these adaptations channel air flow in a way that allows for silent flight, further increasing the owl's hunting prowess, and for Owl People, embracing silence will feature prominently in their journey.

Just because an Owl Person can see so much of what others try to conceal does not mean that they can see *everything*. Even Owl People, with their prodigious capabilities, are unlikely to accurately grasp the entire picture at once. I often describe being clairvoyant and clairaudient as having a whole bunch of puzzle pieces in hand, but while two or three pieces may snap together immediately, I'm not yet sure what to do with the others or even what the eventual picture is supposed to look like. I'm also pretty sure that I'm missing at least half the pieces!

Assembling the puzzle often requires time, patience, and the willingness to surrender my preconceptions to the guidance of the Divine. So it is with Owl People who, if they have not fully matured, may go off half-cocked and either guess the completed picture wrong or reveal things they will later wish they had not (both of which can leave them looking foolish). When an owl hunts, timing is everything; without the adaptation of silent flight, they might give away their presence too soon, and their prey might escape. For Owl People, staying silent until they have all the pieces of the puzzle and have fit them together, and waiting until the time is right to reveal the completed picture, will allow them to achieve the results they desire.

Furthermore, learning how to wait and listen, gathering knowledge over the long term rather than pouncing on the first tidbit they detect, is the difference between an Owl Person being viewed as a know-at-all to be avoided—and becoming a well-respected counselor, healer, and teacher. I am always amazed at the way silence has the power to draw forth the truth of what another is experiencing; in a counseling situation, when we allow for lulls in the conversation and simply wait patiently for another to speak, we give the other person the space in which to admit the things that have been bothering them most. There is a really wonderful quote that goes: "Most people are not listening; they are just waiting for their turn to talk." When we rush to fill the silence with our comments or with our own stories, we make it apparent that we were not truly listening. Silence, then, is an affirmation that yes, what the other person is saying is important, that we want to hear the whole story, and that we will wait while they collect their thoughts and continue. There is so much love in silence, in listening patiently until the other person has finished and is ready to ask for one's wisdom, rather than having it thrust upon them.

Paradoxically, while silence can be a demonstration of love and a willingness to listen, it also has enormous power to make us uncomfortable! I worked in public education for over a decade, and it became apparent very quickly that when a student was lying to me, silence had far more power to draw forth the truth than accusations. I had simply to tell the student that I knew what they had done, then give them a silent stare and respond to all protests to the contrary with an increasingly Vulcan-esque eyebrow-lift. Within a few minutes, outright lies usually turned into excuses, which soon became apologies, promises never to do it again, and pleas for leniency. When an Owl Person becomes adept at wielding silence, they become even better at unearthing that much-desired truth!

Do Not Usually Build Their Own Nests, Most Are Solitary Except During Mating Season

Resulting traits: *Restless * Love to learn and explore * Independent * Fear of commitment to romantic partner*
Resulting lessons: *Accepting themselves for who they are*

Owls nest just about anywhere, but will typically use nests abandoned by other birds or animals rather than building their own. And while several species of owls will mate for life, only a few of those will remain with their partner year-round, choosing instead to reunite only when it is time to breed. Given how casual they seem about their mating place and partner, it may come as a surprise that owls are extremely territorial, viciously attacking other birds, animals, and even humans who stray too close to their nests.

Owl People are naturally active souls, always hungering to explore new places and new concepts, but they must have a safe and familiar place to which they can return to rest and refuel in preparation for their next creative project or journey. They need a place to call home, even if it's only home for part of the time, and they will jealously guard their space from intrusion. Combined with their vulnerability to others' emotions and their subsequent need for alone-time, they are not the sort of people who relish hosting out-of-town guests for more than a day or so at a time. Owl People are not likely to appreciate it if you just "drop in."

In the same way that owls spend long periods of time away from their mates, Owl People tend to have inconsistent relationships with their romantic partners. While most Owl People crave a soul mate with whom to share their lives, they will hesitate over making a commitment that would keep them at that partner's side at all times. Owl People need to be able to come and go as they please, whether this is on a short hike or a journey across the world, and they need to be able to have as much time alone as they desire. Because it takes a particularly adaptable, open-minded soul to be comfortable sharing their lives with someone who requires such flexibility, Owl People often fear they will never find "the right one." Once they accept that they are who they are, and that there is someone out there who will appreciate them, restlessness and all, they will often meet someone who is not only as independent as they are, but who shares their appetite for exploration, and with whom they can comfortably share their adventures.

Swallow Prey Whole, Regurgitate Indigestible Parts

*Resulting traits: Ability to grasp complicated concepts * Not overly attached to physical possessions or relationships that have outlived their usefulness * Require a constant diet of new, stimulating experiences * Confidence * Compassion*

*Resulting lessons: Letting go of situations that are "logical", but not soul-serving * Not letting an attachment to past experiences prevent them from embracing new and different ones * Coping with grief*

Owls swallow their prey whole, then regurgitate the indigestible parts such as the bones, teeth, fur, and claws in the form of pellets (which is one of the reasons people often regret taking an owl for a pet, as happened in the wake of the *Harry Potter* craze). This reflects not only the Owl Person's ability to swallow very large concepts— eagerly tackling the kind of complicated cosmic mysteries that would give the rest of us a headache—but to glean from them the most critical facets without becoming overwhelmed by the nonessential details. Owl People are extremely intelligent.

Additionally, this eating pattern is linked to the Owl Person's ability to discard those things in their lives that do not serve them. Owl People do not tend to be overly sentimental, easily parting with childhood toys, relics of their adolescence or young adulthood, friends to whom they no longer feel connected, and anything else that has outlived its usefulness, provided there is no logical reason for them to do otherwise. There will, of course, be a few meaningful things to which they will hold, but they are most definitely not pack-rats.

Where most of their development will occur, then, is in coping with the loss of those things they do not wish to release. Facts and logic feature prominently in an Owl Person's conscious functioning, and they will often cling to a person, place, or situation because reason says that it should still be good for them, regardless of whether reality is bearing this out. Until they are ready to recognize that when circumstances are no longer meeting their needs, no amount of trying to accept them or force them to be otherwise will make things right, they will remain frustrated, unhappy, and in some cases, physically ill.

Owl People also tend to struggle with letting go of their attachments to enjoyable past experiences. They become fixated on these moments in time and use them to define what they will allow for their future, wanting all new things to happen in the exact same way as the old. New romantic partners cannot be accepted unless they enter the Owl Person's life in precisely the same way as their first, new places to live cannot be explored unless they are discovered in the same fashion as an earlier and much-enjoyed location, a new job cannot be obtained unless it comes to them through the same channels as the first job they loved. Their egos, seeking safety in feelings of control, want them to believe that if new things happen in the same way as the old, it will guarantee that they will be as happy as they were in the old circumstances. Unfortunately, nothing could be further from the truth. Owls cannot eat new food while the pellet created from the old food remains in their system. For Owl People, this means that they *must* let go of the past in order to allow themselves to enjoy a nourishing future; as long as they stay stuck in old beliefs about how things have to occur, new things simply cannot be digested. This is a difficult lesson to learn and once again places an emphasis on the Owl Person's need to cultivate an attitude of flexibility. It is only through being open to *all kinds* of experiences coming to them in *all kinds* of ways that they can live truly vibrant, full lives.

Unlike most other birds, owls do not possess a crop, a sack located near the throat into which birds can store food to be eaten later. The crop is particularly useful when the bird notices a predator before it has had a chance to eat its fill, as it can shove an enormous quantity of food into the pouch, then fly off without having to wait for the food to digest. When it lands and it is again safe, it can then eat the food at its leisure. Lacking this ability, the Owl has no choice but to eat as much as it can when it can, and when it needs more food, to go out and catch more. For Owl People, this once again highlights the need to release their attachment to past experiences and remain eternally willing to welcome the new. Some people can "live" off of a few exceedingly noteworthy experiences their whole lives, mentally and emotionally revisiting them when they are feeling depleted and feeling freshly revitalized or inspired as a result. Not so Owl People. Owl People require a *steady* diet of novel experiences to be happy and healthy. Once it's over, it's over, and they must go forth and seek something new to nourish their spirits. Constant stimulation is as necessary to the Owl Person as breathing.

With all of the emphasis on letting go, it should not be surprising that in the Owl Person's life, navigating through grief is also a frequent theme. Owl People tend to experience more than their share of loss, with some of these losses being traumatic ones. Later on, Owl People often recognize that this loss—however heartbreaking—was something that needed to occur in order for them to move forward in their lives and become the best and strongest possible version of themselves, but they can only get to this point if they allow themselves to embrace their grief and feel it fully so that it may be released. Otherwise, they stay locked in mourning what is gone and never move forward at all. How can they? It is impossible to live in the present or conceive of the future when one is still living in the past.

Surviving and thriving in the wake of loss is a large part of what helps the Owl Person become the confident, independent creature they were created to be. Too, it is these experiences that help them develop the compassion that can make them such wise counselors. Those most adept at healing the suffering of others are most often those who have suffered themselves, and those most capable of giving compassion are most often those who once had great need of it. When they choose to do so, Owl People can become beacons of love.

8 OWL AS A SPIRIT GUIDE

When Owl appears as a spirit guide, it is likely that one or more of the following messages will apply to you. However, it is important to ask yourself how you already relate to owls, as your own experiences matter considerably in interpreting the wisdom of a spirit guide. In other words, if one of the messages below does not apply, it may be that there is a different, more personal meaning of which you are intended to become aware.

For example, if you read the previous edition of this book, you may recall that I referenced a scene from the movie, *My Cousin Vinny*[6]. The movie features a running-gag in which the protagonist constantly has to change where he is staying, because each location features a different startling noise that occurs in the wee hours of the night or morning. In one of my favorite scenes, Vinny expects to finally find

---

[6]*My Cousin Vinny*. Dir. Johnathan Lynn. Writ. Dale Launer. Twentieth Century Fox Film Corporation, 1992.

peace and quiet in an insolated cabin in the woods, only to be abruptly woken by the ear-shattering vocalizations of an Eastern screech owl. It isn't until he finds himself in jail that he is actually able to get some sleep, as despite the calamitous nature of the prison-noises, they remind him of his home in New York City, and are therefore perceived as peaceful rather than jarring. Because this is one of my favorite movies, and because the scene always made me laugh, it affected the way I thought about Owls; whenever I saw them, my first question to myself was whether or not I was in a Vinny-like situation and feeling uncomfortable in my present environment, no matter how pleasing it might physically appear.

And I would still be doing this, if I hadn't recently discovered that while the movie *shows* an Eastern screech owl, the *noise* it produces was actually dubbed in later and is more likely to have come from a barn owl! Considering Owl's emphasis on truth, this couldn't possibly have been more fitting, and it has changed my personal interpretation of Owl's wisdom. Now when I encounter Owl, the first question I will be asking myself is, "No matter how this situation looks, am I somehow being deceived?" Before doing the research for this second edition, it had never occurred to me that this scene might have been a bit of Hollywood gobbledygook, and so I was especially stricken by the truth. This being the case, Owl will now represent a directive to check *every single fact* before believing what I see and hear, regardless of how accurate things may feel, and most especially before sharing any aspect of the situation with others, as I did with readers of the first edition of this book. Owl has always instructed me to look to the truth of a matter, but this experience has given his wisdom a new level of urgency!

Spiritual Messages:

- Are you making sufficient time to be creative? Owl People need a regular creative outlet to be happy and healthy, and so if it has been awhile since you have engaged your creative abilities, it's time to *make* time to do so! Or, if you are not normally a creative individual, Owl may be suggesting that you explore this side of yourself. Ask yourself what kind of creative project feels *exciting* for you, or especially relaxing. It may be something as simple as coloring in a coloring book, or as complicated as learning how to be a glass-blower. The key is to pick something that makes you feel eager to get started.

- Are you feeling exhausted, cranky, anxious, or otherwise out-of-sorts? You may be spending too much time in the company of others, particularly those who want to cry on your shoulder or who are experiencing a lot of drama. Owl's presence is often an indicator that we are absorbing others' negative emotions, and the fastest way to stop doing this—and allow those emotions to exit our system—is to take a break from other people. It is also helpful to avoid phone calls and texting until you feel better.

- Are you confused about why you feel the way that you do? Or do you notice that you're constantly on an emotional roller-coaster and can't seem to find any peace? It's likely that you are analyzing your emotions or attempting to repress them rather than feeling them. It may be that you do not feel like you *should* have these emotions, or that the emotion is so painful you don't *want* to have it. Nevertheless, we have emotional reactions to things for a reason; they give us important information about the way in which we are experiencing a situation, as well as what may need to change (whether this is a part of the situation itself, or simply our attitude) in order for us to feel better. If we ignore our emotions, we tend to recreate the same situations over and over again, and to therefore feel the same way over and over. We are also more likely to feel stressed, depressed, angry, and lose touch with what we really want. Owl is always a powerful reminder to seek the truth within ourselves first, and there is no more direct path to our Truth than to acknowledge and honor what we are really feeling.

- Are you sufficiently in touch with your maternal side? Are you wanting to nurture others, but do not feel that you have an outlet for your love? If so, ask yourself what population you feel most called to nurture. Children? The elderly? The homeless? The ill? Animals? Find a place that will allow you to volunteer with this population, or simply make an effort to help out where you can (Go to your local animal shelter and play with the residents, for example).

- Are you sufficiently in touch with your femininity? No matter your biological sex or gender-preference, if you have been considering exploring your feminine side—whether this is a way of dress; a way of behaving; oft-labeled "feminine" activities such as knitting, cooking, or dancing; or anything else that feels distinctly *female*, Owl would encourage you to do so. Being willing to explore these portions of ourselves does not mean that we must make these things a permanent part of our being or behaving; it simply means that we give ourselves permission to play and be curious! Something entirely unexpected may arise from this exploration, such as a "man's man" discovering that he loves baking, or a tomboy realizing that she loves ballet. Owl can also encourage gay or bisexual men who are struggling with the truth of their identities to stop trying to force themselves to adhere to the traditional, restrictive definition of "manliness" and instead allow themselves to be their *own* version. Engaging in feminine activities or interests does not make one any less of a man; only one's own self-judgment can do that.

- Owls are extremely territorial and aggressively defend their nests from all potential intruders. Do you feel as though someone is invading your space? Or are you feeling conflicted about allowing someone into your home? Listen to your gut on both accounts; if you feel as though your space is being invaded, it is time to clarify your boundaries. And if you are experiencing reluctance over giving someone access to your home, wait until you know them better and are certain that you can trust them.

- Really pay attention to your environment, particularly auditory cues, as the Universe may use these to direct your focus somewhere important. Even small signs and sounds can have great meaning for you. What are you seeing? Hearing? What do these things suggest about your current circumstances?

- If you are feeling like someone may be attempting to deceive you about their motives or feelings, or as though they are hiding something, you are likely to be correct. Pay attention to these feelings, and don't make frivolous commitments to people you suspect of being duplicitous. Conversely, *you* may be the one who is concealing things at this time. Are you hiding things from others? From yourself? **What truth are you avoiding?**

- Do you feel that it would be best for you to do things a certain way, but other people keep telling you that you must be wrong? For example, do you feel your best when you eat whole grains and lots of fruit, but a friend keeps insisting that you must go gluten-free and avoid all sugar, because that's what works for *her*? Listen to YOURSELF, not to your friend, nor anyone else. You are the only one who really knows what is good for you.

- Are you finding yourself preoccupied with the idea that someone is "getting away with something?" Are you constantly wishing that others would find out the truth about this person, or that they would admit that they are hiding something? Do you feel like the situation just isn't fair? Unless it is *actually your responsibility* to expose the truth, let it go, and let karma do its job. The Universe has a way of making sure that the truth about people comes to light, and you're only making yourself unhappy by obsessing over it.

- If you keep getting gut-feelings about something, even if they are relatively minor, *do not ignore them!* We often ignore gut-feelings, because we are afraid of what it would mean if we took them seriously. If you are doing this, Owl is telling you that it is critical that you gather your courage and listen, because while it may be difficult to acknowledge what these feelings are telling you, and you may have hard choices to make afterwards, the consequences will be far worse if you simply continue to ignore them.

- If you feel stuck in your life, ask yourself where you are refusing to be flexible. It is rare that we find ourselves *truly* stuck; more often than not, we are simply clinging to old notions about how things have to be, or about what we think we must have in order to be happy. Once we allow ourselves to bend just the *slightest* bit, things often begin to move again (and when they don't, it is usually an indicator that we need to be even *more* flexible, in which case, ask yourself a second time where you could release some of your attachment to doing things a certain way or needing something specific).

- If you are experiencing a heightened sense of pressure to do something *right now*, take a step back and reassess. Don't act—or speak—until you are *absolutely* certain the time is right and that you have a complete understanding of the situation at hand.

- If you are considering revealing the truth about someone just to hurt them, or just because it will make you feel good about yourself to do so, *don't*. Step back and ask yourself why you feel the need to do this. What is missing in your life that you would need to wound someone else to feel better about yourself? In most cases, we feel this way when we are being too hard on ourselves, or when we resent someone else for being happy when we are not. In the end, we are the only ones responsible for our happiness, so how can you take ownership of feeling happy? How can you love yourself more? How can you better meet your needs? Again, Owl is calling you to release old attachments and be flexible. This is an urgent message to start taking better care of yourself.

- Do you often offer advice to others when you have not been asked to do so? Do you consistently feel the need to point out others' flaws or failings? Even when you are doing these things as an act of love, it is possible that your comments are not being received in the same spirit with which they were given. Step back, focus on *you*, and let others take care of themselves. Giving people this kind of space will help them see you as loving and understanding rather than judgmental. Then, when they really need help, they will be more willing to ask you for it.

• If you are considering becoming a counselor of any kind, or a healer, Owl may be reminding you that the ability to genuinely listen is the most important skill to develop (In some cases, simply knowing that someone *hears us* when we are in pain is sufficient to immediately release a long-held trauma or physical ailment). In your day-to-day conversations, notice how much you are actually *listening*, and how much you are simply waiting for your turn to speak. This is excellent practice for working with clients, and it also tends to show you how invested your friends are in *you*! When you begin taking time to listen to others, you may notice that others aren't really listening to you; this can be extremely disheartening, but this is also good practice for becoming a counselor or healer, when you must take yourself and your own needs completely out of the equation. This is also an excellent time to work on becoming comfortable with silence; rather than beginning to speak as soon as the other person pauses, wait a few seconds in case they have anything else to add. This is truly the mark of a good listener. Too, because silence can also make people uncomfortable enough that they say things they didn't originally intend to say just to relieve the pressure, it's also a good way to get people to confess their true feelings about something, or to admit to telling a lie.

- You, yourself, may be in need of someone to hear you. If you do not have a friend or family member you can trust, seek out a therapist, counselor, or healer that resonates with your needs. All of us need help sometimes, and there is no shame in asking for it! Do allow yourself to get hung up on details such as not having insurance or sufficient funds; there are many free resources out there that provide a listening ear to those in need, and you will find the one best for you if you remain open-minded and trust your heart to guide you.

- Are you bored? Do you keep telling yourself that you should be fine, because you have so many things to do, but nothing is satisfying you? Owl People need constant mental stimulation and a steady diet of new experiences to be healthy and happy, and so Owl's arrival often indicates that our lives have become stale! How can you invigorate your life? What changes could you make? What new things could you learn? Where could you travel? You don't need to do anything dramatic—just look for whatever makes you feel excited or inspired, and do what you can to make it happen. Even something as simple as adding a walk in the park each evening, reading a book from a different genre, or trying a new creative activity may be enough to break the monotony.

- Owl helps us to eliminate those aspects of our life that are not nourishing us. Focus on getting the unhealthy stuff—the judgments, habits, perceptions, old wounds, and fears that are preventing you from moving forward—out of your life. This will allow you to heal and grow. Similarly, if a life-circumstance such as a job, relationship, living situation, or commitment to a college or other kind of education isn't bringing you the joy that logic says that it *should*, it is time to reevaluate its role in your life. Letting go may be hard, but it is often only through letting go that we discover what truly makes us happy.

- If you are experiencing a loss, *let yourself grieve, and do so for as long as you need.* It is your right. More, refusing to grieve does not mean that we do not grieve—it means that we never *stop* grieving, and are then unable to move forward in our lives. Allow yourself to feel the trauma and ache of loss, and one day, it will not hurt so much, and you will be able to feel happy again. And in the mean time, be patient and loving with yourself. Moving through grief can be a long road indeed, and you are doing the best that you can.

- I am often asked if seeing an owl is a message that one –or someone that one loves—is about to die or suffer a great misfortune, as this belief is found in many cultures across the globe. Self-fulfilling prophecies aside (If you really believe that Owl is a terrible omen and worry ceaselessly about this, you are indeed more likely to create trouble for yourself), Owl is most often trying to show us where we are deceiving ourselves, or where others are deceiving *us*. Owl is a very serious messenger, and sometimes, it is indicating that these deceptions are preventing us from recognizing that someone is ignoring a truth to such a degree that it is literally about to kill them. I will never forget receiving a message from a young Native American woman who was terrified of Owls and informed me angrily that they were messengers of death. Her brother, she said, was visited by Owls over and over throughout his teens, and then he died in a car accident in his early twenties. He was driving under the influence of drugs, crossed the median, and was hit head-on by a truck. While her fear and anger were understandable, what she refused to consider was that the Owls may not have been harbingers of her brother's foreordained early demise, but repetitive attempts by the Universe to get him to change his reckless behavior before it did indeed get him killed.

We all know when we are refusing to face a truth about ourselves: We notice a physical change that frightens us, but are afraid to see a doctor or healer. We can see the warning signs that our job is about to be eliminated, but it feels easier to just pretend that everything is okay. We see the way we behave towards our family when we are drinking, and we hate hurting them, but we don't think we could survive *without* the alcohol, and so we refuse to seek treatment. It is the same with those we love; most of us do not give ourselves anywhere near enough credit for being intuitive and being at least vaguely aware that something is wrong. When those we love are on a dangerous path, we *do* tend to know—we're just afraid to admit it to ourselves, or the other person refuses to play ball when we ask them about it, and so we decide we must be wrong. If we have been noticing Owl during this time, and then the inevitable consequences of ignorance occur, whether this is a job-loss, a car-accident, an illness, or even death—then we may mistakenly assume that Owl was telling us that something terrible was coming. But the truth is, Owl was trying to tell us that we had the power to *stop* that terrible thing from happening, if we could be brave enough.

• Different kinds of owls represent different messages, so an examination of the habits and adaptations unique to that species will provide you with additional insight into your current situation. The significance of the eight owls about which I am most often asked is detailed in the following chapter.

Physical Messages:

Physical symptoms are often indicators of emotional imbalance. By addressing these emotions and releasing them, it is often the case that the body heals as well.

• Pay attention to your neck. If your neck is stiff or sore, Owl may be telling you that you are limiting your thinking and refusing to look at the whole picture.

What are you avoiding seeing? In what way have you convinced yourself that there is only *one way* things can be? Remember, one of the key words for Owl is "flexibility!"

• Neck and shoulder tension can also be indicators that we are repressing our emotions instead of feeling them. If you tune into yourself and discover that you are feeling fear, anger, guilt, sadness, or any other unpleasant emotion, it's time to give yourself permission to really sit with those feelings and let them speak to you. Some people are able to do this in silence, some through journaling, some through artwork or music, and some through speaking their feelings aloud to a friend or counselor. Keep in mind that giving yourself permission to voice these feelings is not the same as *complaining*; you aren't a victim of your feelings. Rather, your feelings are telling you how you are experiencing your life and what you can release and/or change to improve your experience. With that in mind, speaking about our feelings should always be done with the intention of eventually letting them go.

• The neck and shoulders are also one of the areas in which we harbor feelings of self-judgment. If your neck is stiff or hurts, it's very likely that you are being too hard on yourself. Ask yourself why you think you have to do or be all these things. What fears are driving you? Can you let them go and just trust yourself? If not, sit with your fear until it melts into understanding. It may take awhile to get there, but this is a far more productive use of your time and energy than ceaselessly berating yourself.

- The success of the owl's digestive system is dependent upon constantly eliminating those parts of its meal that are not nourishing (bones, teeth, claws, fur). Unless it does this, it cannot eat anything new. If you are experiencing stomach pains or digestive or eliminatory issues, what feelings, beliefs, traumas, or worn out situations are you refusing to release? What worries are clogging your system? What is so awful that you resent having to "stomach" it? These things are preventing you from moving joyfully through your life, and from welcoming new experiences.

- Owls expel pellets after every meal because the bones, teeth, claws, and fur from their prey *cannot* be digested. If you are prone to vomiting (even if this is due to frequent bouts of food poisoning or influenza), this may be your body's way of telling you that you are trying to force yourself to "stomach" parts of your life that are simply toxic for you. This could be a job that you hate, a relationship that makes you feel terrible, feelings of guilt or shame that you haven't been able to face, or something else that literally makes you sick. Ask yourself what people/things/situations in your life you keep trying to *force* yourself to accept, and then start letting them go! We are not intended to suffer; if something in your life is poisoning you, there *is* a way to extricate yourself. Owl is the truth-seeker above all, and when we are continuing to try to force ourselves to accept something that is so toxic for us that we are literally vomiting it up, we are refusing to examine our situation with the eyes of Truth. Be brave, be compassionate with yourself, and take an honest look at your life. Something needs to change.

- Have you been experiencing difficulties with your toes? In owls, the ability to pivot one of their toes from front to back allows them to grip their prey until they can safely stop and eat it; without this ability, their source of nourishment might wriggle free! In humans, breaking, stubbing, spraining, cutting, or otherwise damaging our toes, or developing warts or cysts, are usually indicators that we feel that Something or Someone is preventing us from obtaining something we need to be healthy and happy. We become fixated on this person or thing as the source of our "stuckness", and we blame and ruminate instead of looking for options. Take a few steps back from the situation and look at the *whole* picture. Is this person/thing *really* the block that you think it is, or are there other alternate paths that you could try if you were willing to be a bit more flexible?

9 SPECIES-SPECIFIC TOTEM CHARACTERISTICS AND MESSAGES

At present, there are approximately 220 known species of owls[7]. In this chapter, you will find additional species-specific information pertaining to eight of the owls about which I am asked most often. If the owl with which you resonate most strongly is other than one of those listed here, a personal study of your Owl's physical characteristics and unique adaptations may assist you in interpreting its wisdom.

The characteristics listed for each specific Owl should be applied in addition to those already discussed as applying to Owl in general.

BARN OWL
Additional totem characteristics:

---

[7] The "exact" number of owl species in the world varies on average between 211 and 222, depending on the source.

- The barn owl's uniquely heart-shaped face is an adaptation designed to improve its hearing, and it gives the barn owl a superior ability to detect prey through sound alone. In fact, barn owls not only have the best hearing of any owl, but some of the best hearing of any animal ever tested! On the one hand, this makes Barn Owl People outstandingly clairaudient; they readily experience guidance through auditory means such as music and random sounds (which may or may not be audible to others), and are more likely to hear spoken words from their guides and have dreams that include memorable words or phrases. However, this extreme psychic sensitivity to sound also means that listening to someone lie to them can actually be physically painful! These individuals are *so* sensitive to the hidden truths behind what someone else is saying that to be in the presence of someone who is saying something that they do not actually believe is a lot like being subjected to the infamous screech of nails on a chalkboard. When a Barn Owl Person finds themselves in conversation with someone and notices that they are feeling angry, anxious, or ill, this is often a signal from their Higher Self that the other person's words are not aligned with their true thoughts or intentions!

- The barn owl's white, mask-like face lends Barn Owl People a serene quality, even if what is going on inside them is quite the opposite. This makes it especially difficult for other people to read a Barn Owl Person's feelings and intentions. If you are a Barn Owl Person, don't assume that people know when you need help or can accurately read your feelings—to others, you will tend to consistently come across as calmer and more collected than you actually are. This being the case, if you need help, ask. If you think someone has not understood your true feelings or needs, make a point of clarifying them. Yes, it can be frustrating to always have to explain ourselves, but it beats the drama that tends to result from miscommunication!

- Unlike most other birds, barn owls cannot store body fat, and so a harsh, cold winter will often result in the owl freezing or starving to death. In this context, the ability to store body fat is comparable to the storing up of "nourishment" from old experiences, i.e., being able to mentally revisit previous experiences and receive a fresh dose of joy or excitement. In general, most Owl People cannot survive on memory alone; to be happy and healthy, they must continually seek out novel experiences to inspire and invigorate them. In Barn Owl People, however, this is *especially* pronounced, with a long-term absence of fresh mental and emotional stimulation resulting in depression, apathy, exhaustion, and, if permitted to continue, physical malaise and even death. Barn Owl People really *can* be "bored to death!" These individuals must therefore make continuous learning and exploration a priority, whether this means reading books, trying new hobbies, taking classes, or enjoying invigorating conversations with friends.

- Though barn owls possess extraordinarily sensitive hearing that can be easily overwhelmed by ambient noise, they still make the frequent choice to nest and roost in very noisy places, such as church bell towers and drive-in movie screens! Similarly, while Barn Owl People are easily overwhelmed by the intense energies of others, and while they tend towards a more introverted personality, they still enjoy being *around* other people. Simply sitting in a corner observing others and listening to their conversations can be a great deal of fun for them.

Additional spirit guide messages:

- Pay particular attention to what you are hearing at this time, both while you are awake and when dreaming, as this is the fashion in which your guidance is most likely to appear. Even random sounds may have significant meaning.

- Do not trust a person or situation solely on account of what someone says—listen with your gut, not your mind, as this is how you will recognize when something is being incorrectly represented or is going unspoken.

- Other people may be having trouble interpreting how you feel unless you actually spell it out for them. Be especially clear about your needs, feelings, and beliefs, and do not simply assume others understand what is going on with you.

- If you are feeling the urge to stay up past your normal bedtime, do so! You are likely to do your best work at this time.

- If you have been feeling depressed or apathetic, it's a good bet that you are bored! Depression in particular is often the result of being bored or unhappy with our lives, but feeling as though we are powerless to make the necessary changes. And so again and again, we think of something that would feel stimulating or exciting, and again and again we tell ourselves this is not possible, until we arrive at a place of feeling utterly defeated. And when we feel defeated, it's tough to find the motivation to do *anything!* If you are feeling this way, it's time to start making some changes! Stop making excuses or telling yourself that you can't do the things that excite you, and begin finding ways to make them happen. Even small changes are wholly worthwhile, as they put you in a more positive frame of mind, and from this more positive place, you are able to connect with what is needed to create the bigger changes. No matter what anyone has told you, you are not meant to feel consistently unfulfilled.

BARRED OWL
Additional totem characteristics:

- The barred owl does not migrate, instead remaining year-round in the same area in which it was born and raised. For Barred Owl People, having a safe, comfortable place to call home is of special import, and they will rarely demonstrate the same restlessness as other Owl People. These individuals will tend to be happiest being at or near their homes, whatever adventures they take occurring on more of a mental level than a physical one.

- Barred owls are sit-and-wait predators; they choose a place to perch, wait patiently, then dive after whatever wanders too close. As a result, mature Barred Owl People tend to be the kind for whom whatever they want eventually just falls in their laps, and it is the Barred Owl Person's attitude that will determine whether this makes for a pleasant life or a frustrating one. It will only be the former if the Barred Owl Person has cultivated an attitude of trust that what they want will always be provided, the patience to wait for it, and the awareness to recognize its appearance. Otherwise, they can worry themselves sick fretting over when and how something will manifest, or they can exhaust themselves attempting to go after it.

- Barred owl parents care for their young for a much longer period than most other owls, sometimes for up to six months. In Barred Owl People, this can often reflect a lack of confidence—a feeling that they just aren't ready to be on their own and take care of themselves! When this is the case, it is important for them not to *avoid* adult responsibilities or new adventures, but to remember that they do not have to do these things alone; there is no shame in asking for guidance as they learn new things. The lengthy time spent raising their chicks can also mean that Barred Owl People themselves become especially invested in raising their children, wanting to make sure that their little ones are absolutely ready to be out on their own before they let them go. Provided that this does not turn into smother-mothering—not letting one's children take any risks at all, no matter how age-appropriate—Barred Owl People can make the most conscientious and loving of parents, attentive to their children's needs and encouraging of their growth.

Additional spirit guide messages:

- If you are feeling anxious or stressed, it may be that you are moving around too much! If you are always going out to dinner, order a pizza (or whatever else can be delivered in your area), or make a home-cooked meal. If your job requires a hectic commute or regular travel, it may be time to take a few days off and just enjoy staying home! If you do not feel that you have a permanent home, it may be time to begin looking for a place to settle down. Look to your birthplace first (or a place that resembles it), as this location is most likely to offer you the greatest comfort.

- If you are debating between two or more options that differ in their physical proximity to your current location (such as a job that it is within driving distance, verses one that would require you to relocate), the arrival of Barred Owl would advise you to select the closer option.

- If you are stressing yourself out trying to figure out how to obtain something you desire, it's time to stop trying to think yourself to your goal and start listening for guidance. Barred Owl's appearance often indicates that those things that we want will simply fall in our laps, and all we must do is be open and aware when they do! You may be spinning your wheels to such a degree that you have been unable to hear your intuition telling you how to get where you want to go, or you may have been forcing action when all the necessary parts have yet to align, and so it is not actually *possible* for you to have what you want at this time. Take a break from trying to mentally solve the issue, and sit and wait quietly. Your answer will come, even if it is simply that you need to sit and wait a little longer (and while this is usually the last answer that we want to receive, everything really *does* occur in the perfect way and time when we stop trying to control the process).

- You may feel that you are not ready for something, as though you'd feel much better if there were someone there to hold your hand! If this is the case, ask for guidance or further clarification; you don't have to do this all by yourself right now. On the other hand, if you feel as though you really want to do something by yourself but another party is insisting that you need further guidance, give the other party their due and listen to what they have to say. They are likely acting in your best interests and have valuable wisdom to share. You'll be ready to go it alone soon enough.

BURROWING OWL
Additional totem characteristics:

- Unlike other owls, who nest in trees or on the ground, burrowing owls nest *under*ground, either in holes dug by other burrowing creatures such as prairie dogs, or less frequently, in dens they have excavated themselves. This type of nesting pattern creates individuals who tend to be especially anxious about their perceived level of vulnerability. Nothing frightens a Burrowing Owl Person more than the idea that someone might be able to look deeply inside them while they are helpless to stop it. They need to feel that they have the ability to control who sees how much of them and to able to escape when the scrutiny of others becomes uncomfortable or overwhelming. These people not only like their privacy, they *require* it in order to feel safe. Ironically, Burrowing Owl People are some of the most instinctively inquisitive souls out there—from the instant they meet you, they are taking you apart, trying to figure out how you work. But the idea that someone might be doing this to them when they do not *want* to reveal their inner-workings is extremely frightening, and so they will often flee (or put up some pretty hefty walls!) when they note others taking too pointed an interest in them.

- Living in underground burrows rather than in above-ground nests also makes Burrowing Owl People more aware of the practical demands of life (the "earth"-related aspects), most especially those involving money. Financial security is extremely important to these individuals, particularly in the form of a reliable, predictable income. However, like the burrows that can collapse or flood, the notion of a "reliable" income provides a false sense of security. No job is guaranteed forever. Burrowing Owl People need to remember that their security is not in their jobs, but in *themselves*, and in their ability to trust their hearts to guide them to the money that they need. Otherwise, they can become so convinced that they require a certain job to maintain their financial security that they will refuse to leave it, even when the job is no longer meeting their needs or has become completely unpleasant. If they wait too long, what they perceive as their financial safe haven—their "burrow"—may collapse around them.

- Burrowing Owl People are the most mentally and emotionally grounded of the Owl People, which allows for an easier time engaging in self-exploration. They tend to become aware of internal imbalances more quickly, and to be able to address them with less effort. And though they are still subject to intense emotions, these emotions do not occur to the same extreme degree as with other Owl People, nor do they cycle so rapidly between them.

- Burrowing owlets are uniquely adapted to protect themselves when Mommy and Daddy are away; when they sense a predator outside the burrow, they make a sound that mimics a rattlesnake! Rather than a hole filled with soft, fluffy snacks, the predator now thinks it has stumbled across the den of a deadly snake, and it is going to think twice about attempting to stick its head or paw in there. Similarly, Burrowing Owl People are exceptionally sweet, vulnerable souls; it would not take much to wound them very gravely. However, they know how to make all the right noises to get others to think that they are far stronger and more confident than they really are.

- Burrowing Owls are exceptionally clever and versatile hunters, able to hover, grab their prey mid-flight, dive from a perch and snatch their prey from the ground, or run after grasshoppers and beetles on foot. They will even deposit mammal dung around their burrows as bait for dung beetles, which are one of their favorite foods. It is impossible to pigeon-hole a Burrowing Owl Person—they just won't do things the same way every time and can always generate a new approach if an old one isn't working. Too, this versatility makes Burrowing Owl People uniquely flexible when it comes to their hobbies and careers. Multi-talented, these individuals are likely to have a large assortment of creative and stimulating past-times, and when they release their security-worries sufficiently to change jobs when the need arises, these changes often place them in entirely different careers. These are the sorts of people who go to school to be an engineer, but then spend ten gleeful years as a florist, and then one day decide to quit flowers and open a food truck specializing in Creole-Hungarian fusion.

- Unlike other owls, who are mostly solitary except during mating season, burrowing owls often nest in loose colonies. Burrowing Owl People may require privacy, but they are not hermits; most would be lonely if they were completely isolated. Too, they enjoy the process of figuring out what makes others tick far too much! These individuals function best when they are surrounded by other people like themselves who need privacy but enjoy knowing that company is there when they want it (I often imagine Burrowing Owl People as the sort who would enjoy living in an art colony. Many artists are private, introverted souls, but who enjoy being in the aura of other creative spirits like themselves).

- In addition to its unique living space, burrowing owls are readily identifiable by the delightfully comical way in which they bob and tilt their heads, as though they are attempting to examine someone or something from *all* possible angles. Owl People as a whole love to do this, but Burrowing Owl People take it to an entirely new level. One of my clients, the divine Burrowline of Paris, France, described this tendency beautifully, saying, " . . . If I am not careful, I'll push the process so far that I'll get a bit lost in it, and no longer be able to tell where my own standpoint is, or no longer want to stand by it because it feels way too narrow. This can lead to people feeling like I can't or won't have an opinion about things. But to me, it simply feels like just one standpoint covers way too little of the matter to be meaningful. Everything is so relative." Burrowing Owl People simply cannot stop looking at every angle until they have run out of angles to explore, partially because they would hate to risk making an uninformed—or unfair!—decision, and partially because the exploration is a joy unto itself!

Additional spirit guide messages:

- If you are feeling especially anxious, it may be that you feel that your physical or emotional privacy is being violated. If your emotional privacy is the issue, it is important to remember that you do not have to answer people's probing questions simply because they have asked them; you are in complete control of what and how much you share. You also do not have to allow people into your personal space! If you feel that your physical boundaries are being overstepped, it is completely okay to tell someone that they are standing too close to you or that no, you do not wish to be hugged or touched. And if you are dealing with a situation in which you simply do not have any privacy (in an open office, for example), make sure to secure enough alone-time to let your system release the effects of having been overtaxed by the presence of others.

- If you have been worried about money, or have been forcing yourself to stay in a job that you do not enjoy because you believe that it is the source of your financial security, Burrowing Owl would suggest that you reevaluate this belief. Most burrowing owls do not dig their own burrows; they simply dash in and claim one that was already made. Similarly, if you are staying in a job you do not enjoy, it's okay to take a risk and find another! There is probably one just waiting for you, just as there is usually a burrow ready and waiting for the hopeful burrowing owl. And if you look around and cannot find a job that you want, consider creating your own! Remember, our financial security is not in our jobs, but in *US*. YOU are the source of your income, and if you allow your intuition to lead you, you will connect with money-making opportunities that are enjoyable, make the best use of your talents, and meet your financial needs. This same advice applies if you have been staying in a home that you do not enjoy, but are afraid to search for another. Open yourself up to intuitive guidance (meaning, do what *feels* good with regard to your home-search, rather than what makes logical sense), and you will be directed to a home that meets your needs.

- Whatever situation you are currently dealing with is likely calling for a good dose of flexibility and innovation. If you are stalled in a project or decision, try to approach it from another angle, and be willing to try something radically different. And if you are still stuck, try calling in a fresh set of eyes. Another person may be able to see something that you are missing.

- Burrowing owls are the only owls that nest in colonies and really seem to enjoy each other's company. If you have been feeling out of sorts, spending time with a group of zany, like-minded folks like yourself may be just what you need!

- Do not allow people to force you into making a decision with which you are not comfortable, just because they are impatient. It is okay for you to thoroughly ponder every aspect of the situation—and to change your mind as much as you need—before you arrive at the course that feels best to you. Just make sure to remain aware of how you are feeling during this process; if you begin to feel anxious about selecting the correct course rather than excited or intrigued by all the possibilities, it's an indicator that you have lost touch with your intuitive connection to the best path. Take a step back from thinking and start asking which course *feels* best.

EURASIAN EAGLE OWL
Additional totem characteristics:

- The Eurasian eagle owl is one of the largest known owl species, weighing up to 9 lbs (4 kg) with a wingspan of up to 6 ft (2 m). On account of its size and strength, it has no natural enemies, yet it still falls prey to the perils of inattention and/or ignorance, namely electrocution via power lines, collision with traffic, and being shot by hunters. Eurasian Eagle Owl People are extremely intelligent and are usually quite aware of their own power, so it is not difficult for them to develop a false sense of security about the way in which they move through the world. This variety of Owl Person is one of those most prone to living on "auto-pilot", ignoring intuitive signals that might be warning them that they are on a "collision-course" with something unpleasant. They may be less likely to be attacked outright than other people, and they may have the intellectual chops to solve the most baffling problems, but they still need to listen to their Higher Self when it warns them that an attack or problem might be forthcoming! This way, they can get out of the way if possible or prepare themselves if not, rather than being forced to confront it head-on when they least expect it. When a Eurasian Eagle Owl Person's intuition tells them that something is "off", they need to give that signal their immediate and undivided attention.

- While Eurasian eagle owls are ferocious hunters, and there have been several accounts of Eurasian eagle owl attacks on humans, on the whole, these owls generally shy away from people, rather than attack them as great horned owls and barred owls have been known to do. Too, falconers and those who work with these owls at rehabilitation centers overwhelmingly describe them as unexpectedly good-natured, delighting in being stroked and petted, even by excited children. Mature Eurasian Eagle Owl People may seem intimidating, and they are certainly powerful, but they understand the proper use of this power, being aggressive when appropriate and gentle when not. And if you are a Eurasian Eagle Owl person who has a difficult time connecting with others, it is likely because people can sense your inherent power and are afraid of you! Making friends, therefore, may require an especially proactive approach on your part, starting conversations yourself, for example, instead of waiting to be approached, or seeking out social groups of like-minded others who share your interests, rather than simply hoping to encounter one somewhere.

- The prodigious size and strength of the Eurasian eagle owl give those for whom this is a totem the ability to rise effortlessly to the top of whatever vocation they choose. Additionally, because each owl in a Eurasian eagle owl population has its own distinct voice and can be reliably identified by its vocalizations alone, Eurasian Eagle Owl People are especially unique. When they apply their power to a creative pursuit, the fruits of their labor will tend to be wonderfully different from anything else in existence.

- Eurasian eagle owls will eat almost anything that moves, from bugs to baby deer. For Eurasian Eagle Owl People, this represents being possessed of an exceptionally wide range of interests. These individuals tend to be fascinated by so many different subjects that they can keep a conversation fresh and interesting for hours on end.

Additional spirit guide messages:

- If you have been getting the feeling that something is wrong, *listen to it*. Regardless of how good things may "look" in your life, your intuition is probably trying to tell you that you are refusing to acknowledge something that could come back to bite you later.

- If you are having a difficult time making friends, it may be because others find you intimidating and are frightened to approach you. If this feels like the case, try being the one to start conversations with others instead of waiting for them to come to you. It may also be that you are surrounding yourself with people who are so different from you that they simply cannot relate, in which case, look for ways to meet people more like yourself. Some possible ways to do this could be joining a website like Meetup.com, spending more time in places you enjoy, or taking a class in a subject that interests you.

- Dream as big as you want! Whatever you want to achieve, no matter how far-fetched, it is within your grasp.

- A unique approach will serve you best at this time, no matter the task. Those people who make the biggest impact are never those who do things the way everyone else did them, but those who dare to be different and blaze their own trails.

GREAT GREY OWL
Additional totem characteristics:
- The great grey owl is North America's largest owl and boasts a wingspan of up to sixty inches, yet it is mostly fluff and weighs only two-to-three pounds (.91-to-1.4 kg.)—half the weight of the smaller snowy owl! Great Grey Owl People naturally surround themselves with an aura of confidence, and they will tend to consistently

give the impression that they have it all together even when they are feeling stressed. But this stoic attitude often conceals a very vulnerable soul, and it is important for those with Great Grey Owl as their totem to ask for help when they need it. Otherwise, not only will they remain in need, but they may develop the mistaken impression that no one truly cares about them and their interests. If they want others to be involved in their life, they need to be willing to admit when they are not feeling as strong as they appear.

- Like barn owls, great grey owls possess a pronounced facial disk, which heightens the great grey owl's hearing to an incredible degree and gives the great grey owl a superior ability to detect prey through sound alone. This makes Great Grey Owl People outstandingly clairaudient, with their most significant guidance typically presented through auditory means such as music, random sounds (which may not be audible to others!), or even actual words or phrases spoken by their guides. This also makes them particularly sensitive to whether or not someone is telling the truth; if Great Grey Owl People find themselves feeling angry, anxious, or ill while in conversation with another, it is more likely that the other person's words are not representative of their true feelings or intentions.

- Great grey owls are especially devoted parents. When food is scarce, the female will starve herself in order to provide sufficient food for her chicks, and even after the chicks have left the nest, both parents continue to feed and defend them for several months. The female is the first to leave the family group, with the male remaining to feed the chicks for a few more weeks, at which point they are usually able to capture prey on their own. For Great Grey Owl People, a special importance is placed upon their role as a parent. They take it very seriously and may find themselves making considerable sacrifices for their children (far more than what would be considered "normal"). While being a new parent is a demanding endeavor for anyone, for Great Grey Owl People, it can be simply overwhelming. And yet, they would have it no other way, as their children are their first priority.

• Despite receiving excellent parental care, a great grey owl chick's childhood is not one of idyllic ease; as waste accumulates in the nest, the odor becomes a beacon for predators, and so the chicks are ushered out of the nest by their mothers at the tender age of three-to-four weeks old, tumbling to the ground or climbing down on their own. They are not yet able to fly, but they are excellent climbers, and are able to make their way up nearby trees, where they continue to receive care from their parents for a time. Great Grey Owl People demonstrate unusually high expectations for their children; they do not tolerate laziness, temper-tantrums, or other immature behaviors, but encourage their children to be appropriately mature and to explore their strengths. They feel it is imperative that their children learn how to take care of themselves as quickly as possible, and they will support their children as they learn how to do this. To outsiders (and to the Great Grey Owl Person's children), this may appear as though the children are being forced to grow up before they are ready, but the Great Grey Owl Person typically has a solid understanding of their children's needs and would not push them unduly. On the other hand, you may be a Great Grey Owl Person who feels that your own parents forced you to grow up before you were ready. If this is the case, keep in mind that in doing so, they probably believed that they were doing what was best for you, and that they would not have pushed you if they did not think you could handle it. They may have been wrong—it may have been harder for you than they realized—but they were likely acting in what they believed were your best interests.

- Like great snowy owls, great grey owls often must seize their prey from deep below the snow. In metaphysical terms, snow is representative of "frozen emotions" or numbness, and to nourish themselves, Great Grey Owl People must make a habit of breaking through this barrier and reaching for the warmth (the feelings, both positive and negative) that lies beneath. Exceptionally logical, these people naturally subject everything they experience to a thorough analysis—the second they start to feel something, they want to know why! Their greatest spiritual breakthroughs will come not through critical examination, however, but through quieting their minds and allowing themselves to just *feel* their way towards the truth, trusting their hearts above all.

Additional spirit guide messages:

- If you are going through a stressful time and feel as though no one seems to notice or care about your suffering, be aware that the strong image you are portraying is preventing people from recognizing that you are in need. You are not alone—others simply aren't aware that you do not presently feel as tough or confident as you are pretending to be. If you need help, ask. There are those who wish to help you, but you have to be the initiator.

- Pay particular attention to what you are hearing at this time, as this is the fashion in which your guidance is most likely to appear. Even random sounds may have significant meaning.

- Do not trust a person or situation solely on account of what someone says—listen with your gut, not your mind, as this is how you will recognize when something is being incorrectly represented or is going unspoken.

- If you are feeling overwhelmed by your parental responsibilities, know that this is because you have chosen to be the very best parent that you can be, and that your present level of stress won't last forever. In giving so much of yourself to your children, you are helping them become healthy, happy, and better able to take care of themselves when the time arrives (after which you can relax and congratulate yourself on a job well-done!).

- Do you feel that you are being pushed to grow up too fast, or to do things for which you do not feel ready? It may not seem like it, but you *are* ready to meet these new challenges, and you are far stronger and more resourceful than you realize! You are also likely to have far more support than you are aware of, so if you are struggling, look around for assistance and ask for it!

- Like Great Snowy Owl, Great Grey Owl sometimes arrives to tell us that we are harboring "frozen emotions" around a significant emotional event or trauma. This is especially likely if we are experiencing a physical illness. See my account of Great Snowy Owl Woman's visit in Chapter 11 for guidance on how to approach this kind of situation.

GREAT HORNED OWL
Additional totem characteristics:

- The great horned owl is remarkably strong and can carry off animals many times its own size. By extension, Great Horned Owl People often must endure especially trying circumstances for the sake of spiritual growth, things that would be too weighty for a lesser soul to bear. But no matter how overwhelming their journey may sometimes feel, they are perfectly equipped to not only survive, but to thrive!

- The great horned owl can turn its head a full 270 degrees, the farthest extreme of which an owl species is capable. These individuals can see *all* sides of a story, consider *all* possibilities. While this can make them excellent therapists, counselors, writers, judges, and humanitarians, they can also scare themselves out of taking action because they've thoroughly explored everyone's possible ulterior motives and every possible thing that could go wrong. They don't want to act without *knowing* exactly which choice is the right one, and yet, they can never gain enough knowledge to be certain *enough*. And so many Great Horned Owl People have trouble acting at all, rendered inert by their need to fully understand the outcome before it has occurred.

- When clenched, the great horned owl's grip is so strong that it requires 28 pounds of pressure to open. Great Horned Owl People do not give up once they finally set their sights upon something they want. This determination can help them succeed in the trickiest endeavors, but it can also hold them back, as they may become so attached to doing things in a certain way that they ignore an easier, more effective option, or they become so invested in pursuing a particular course that they are unwilling to acknowledge when it may be leading them astray or may not actually be what they want at all!

- With the two previous points in mind, it should not be surprising that Great Horned Owl People are really here to work on balance, much like those born under the sign of Libra. Somewhere between the drive to analyze every possible facet of a situation and the craving for the security to be found in selecting a course and sticking with it is the voice of their Higher Selves. This voice does not speak in the language of facts and logic, but in the sensation of Knowing without knowing how one Knows. It is *surety* where other voices are constructs of fear. How does one hear this voice? By feeling and releasing all fear, guilt, and other limiting emotions so that only Knowing remains. Great Horned Owl People in particular must learn to feel their way to balance, rather than think it. This does not mean that there is no room in their lives for thinking and analyzing, but that they need to recognize when thinking is only keeping them stuck, and yield to emotion if it is present. When limiting emotions have been released, thought is effortless, and we often simply "arrive" at the conclusions that get us exactly where we want to be.

- Unlike other owls, who avoid preying upon skunks due to the threat of being sprayed, great horned owls make frequent meals of them, and some eat skunks exclusively! This makes Great Horned Owl People more open-minded than many others, able to see the potential for growth and nourishment in people and situations that others might instinctively reject. However, the great horned owl's steady diet of skunk often means that they wind up smelling like them, and in Great Horned Owl People, this behavior is echoed in their tendency to be *so* open-minded about people (usually because they have over-thought the situation, instead of allowing themselves to be guided by their feelings) that they can allow individuals into their lives who are positively toxic, and then become saturated with that negative energy themselves. If they are unable to clear this energy, they may find others avoiding them because they are broadcasting negativity like skunk-stink, much like the way those who rescue injured great horned owls often find the owl must be "aired out" for a little while before the odor fades enough that they can be brought inside and cared for! If Great Horned Owl People notice that their friends are suddenly avoiding them, it would be a good idea for them to do an attitude check. If they are feeling exceptionally icky, their energy may be too overwhelming for others to bear, and they need to spend some time feeling and releasing.

- Other owls will tend to relocate as an act of self-preservation when a great horned owl moves into the area, as these fierce predators are known to take down prey larger than themselves, including ospreys, porcupines, and even other great horned owls. In the Great Horned Owl Person, this translates into the tendency of others to find them thoroughly intimidating. Some Great Horned Owl People will take advantage of this, moving into new environments or social circles and simply taking what the want, regardless of the needs of others. They can occasionally be bullies, aware that their innate power makes it unlikely that people will stand up to them. However, some Great Horned Owl People can act from a place of selfishness and yet be totally unaware that this is what they are doing; they just know that they are intended to have their needs met, and it doesn't occur to them that the lives of others might be disrupted by the Great Horned Owl Persons' desires. And even when they are doing noting whatsoever to disturb others, such is their aura of power that others will still tend to demonstrate a pronounced reaction to their presence. People may avoid them despite their attempts to be friendly, or they may suddenly find themselves mobbed by those who want to make them feel badly about themselves, as crows will often mob great horned owls and attempt to drive them off. It is important for Great Horned Owl People be willing to process their feelings of anger, fear, and loneliness in order to get to the truth of the matter. People may be avoiding them or attacking them because they really *are* doing something to upset others, or others may be acting from a place of insecurity or envy. To know how to handle the issue, they must understand what has created it. Then, they can either choose to change their behavior, speak clearly about their intentions so that others feel less threatened, or, if necessary, "bite" those who would attack them without provocation.

Additional spirit guide messages:

- If times are tough for you right now, hang in there! You are merely experiencing a period of intense growth, and you have everything that you need to make it through and come out better than you were before. Just keep listening to your heart—not your fear!—and love yourself as much as possible, and you will find your way.

- With all endeavors or conundrums at this time, it is crucial to strike a balance between considering *every possible option* and becoming rigidly fixated on just one. If you have been thinking the matter to death, stop. Breathe. *Feel.* Those answers that truly serve us tend to come in the form of Knowing, not logic. So what direction *feels* best (In other words, what would you do if you *knew* that no matter what choice you made, everything would be okay)? Go that way, regardless of whether or not it makes sense. And if you have been fixated on things happening in a specific way, and that way is not working, it's time to loosen up and examine some other options. Either there is another option that will serve you better (and you will know, because the idea will feel good to you, even if it is totally illogical), or that which you want is not intended to manifest at this time. If you really sit and feel your frustration around the situation until the feeling runs out, there is a good chance that you will suddenly Know that all is happening in the perfect time, and that you just need to be patient.

- If you are feeling exhausted, apathetic, pessimistic, moody, anxious, or otherwise less-than-ideal, take an honest look at the people with whom you have most recently had contact. There's a good chance that at least one of them will be the sort who is always needing you to comfort them, or who wants to constantly cry on your shoulder. They are also likely to be the type of person who complains and complains, yet does not do anything to improve their situation. If this is what is happening, then this person is not good for you at this time. You either need to distance yourself from them, or you need to be willing to set personal boundaries and tell them when you do not have the resources to hear or comfort them any longer. Just because someone expresses a need does not mean that you must meet it. Your health and wellness is just as important as theirs.

- If you notice that other people seem to be angry with you, ask yourself if you may have been selfish of late. Have you been going after the things you want without thought to what this may be creating for others? This does not mean to give up on what you want, only to be more aware of how you are going about obtaining it.

- If other people seem to suddenly be attacking you for no apparent reason, chances are that they are perceiving you as intimidating and are feeling insecure. Try not to take it personally, and respond from a place of calm and confidence. Do not allow yourself to be hurt or driven off, however, and if they refuse to be gentled, defend yourself!

- Someone may be encroaching upon your "turf" and trying to take all your resources for themselves. Going up against this person yourself is unlikely to be successful, so if you must confront them, do so with a group of like-minded, supportive others.

GREAT SNOWY OWL

Additional totem characteristics:

- The great snowy owl is easily recognized by its white plumage, and while its coloration ranges from white with dark bars to pure white depending upon the age and gender of the owl, the predominance of white gives Great Snowy Owl people a more intense hunger to experience and understand the spiritual side of their existence. White is the color of the Divine, of love and faith and forgiveness, and to live a genuinely spiritual life is to see the Divine in all things. To know the love of the Divine, however, one must first learn to see and love oneself in the way that the Universe sees and loves one, and to develop enduring faith, one's faith must be tested. For this reason, the Great Snowy Owl Person's journey is among the most difficult there is—a fully realized Great Snowy Owl Person is not a pop-psychologist or self-stylized New Age guru, but the real deal, a person who has faced the abyss and Knows—KNOWS—how to listen to the Divine and surrender to its guidance. And the most obvious indicator that they have reached this point? Silence. A mature Great Snowy Owl Person's greatest teachings tend to come not from speeches or lectures, but as a result of simply being themselves while others observe. Through their own walk with the Divine, others learn what it means to live a life of love and trust.

- Great snowy owls must often seize their prey from deep below the snow. In metaphysical terms, snow is representative of numbness or "frozen" emotions, and while all Owl People tend to be analytical sorts who want to know *why* they are feeling something before they fully allow themselves to experience that feeling, Great Snowy Owl People in particular are more likely to "freeze" their feelings rather than flow with them. Many of these individuals grew up in exceptionally stoic households in which emotional expression was frowned upon, and they only received love and approval when they were "sucking it up" and pretending that everything was okay. In this way, these tender souls often confuse wisdom and maturity with emotional androgyny, making this an especially challenging pattern to break. Nevertheless, when they repress their feelings, these individuals are setting themselves up for rapid spiritual starvation, as the emotions that would tell them what they really need to "nourish" themselves have been locked away. To live a happy, healthy, satisfied life, Great Snowy Owl People must make a regular habit of "breaking through the ice", making a conscious choice to face and feel their emotions rather than push them aside, tell themselves they shouldn't have them, or try to change them. They must learn to accept their feelings *as they are.* The more they do this, the more they will be able to hear the Divine guidance for which they so hunger.

- Great Snowy Owls are one of the more nomadic species of owl, traveling far from their birthplaces and flying hundreds and hundreds of miles each year in search of food. By extension, Great Snowy Owl people are *especially* restless, taking great joy in traveling not just their native countries, but the rest of the world as well. In addition to the more mental delights of traveling to a new location—seeing the sights, meeting new people— each geographic location harbors its own unique energy, and it is largely this energy that excites the Great Snowy Owl Person. For these people, traveling isn't just about seeing what is there, but *feeling* it, receiving nourishment from the land itself. While a Great Snowy Owl Person will tend to have a home-base that they will guard fiercely, this place will rarely meet all of their energetic and intellectual needs, and so travel is a must, rather than a luxury.

- Unlike most other owls, great snowy owls are extremely diurnal, doing the bulk of their hunting in broad daylight rather than in darkness. For Great Snowy Owl People, their most successful work will tend to be accomplished in daylight, and during the times when their Owl totem is most present in their lives, a lack of sufficient sunshine will tend to have a direct effect on their moods and attitudes. Seasonal affective disorder, a variety of depression related to the change in seasons and thought to be linked to lower levels of sunlight, is more likely to affect individuals with this variety of Owl totem (and because there are many natural treatments available to ameliorate this condition, do not worry if this is you—simply talk to your naturopath or holistic healer should you find yourself in need).

Additional spirit guide messages:

- Whatever trial you are experiencing at this time, the Universe is encouraging you to seek resolution through connection with the Divine. This means accepting that every facet of you is worth loving, even when you make mistakes or consider yourself otherwise imperfect. It means giving others the same grace, knowing that even when they hurt you, they are only human and are doing the best that they can. And it means trusting that the Universe wants you to be your most joyful self, and that the way it tells you that you are on the right track is that you *feel* joyful! Move towards the experiences that make your heart sing, and you are moving towards the Divine. This is where all healing lies.

- Great Snowy Owl sometimes arrives to tell us that we are harboring "frozen emotions" around a significant emotional event or trauma. This is especially likely if you are experiencing a physical illness. It may also be that Great Snowy Owl is attempting to help you break a life-long pattern of emotional repression so that you can finally identify your true needs and begin to address them. If you have no idea how to begin feeling your feelings—or are afraid of what doing so might mean—I strongly recommend the book *Letting Go: The Pathway of Surrender* by David R. Hawkins (Hay House, 2014), which explains how and why allowing ourselves to feel our feelings as they occur is key to our health and happiness. You can also see my account of my experience with Great Snowy Owl Woman in Chapter

11 for an example of how to use emotional release to heal from trauma.

- If you are feeling restless or have found yourself wanting to move to a new location, it is likely that your present location is not meeting your needs at this time. Owl People often keep themselves stuck in unfulfilling circumstances because it makes logical "sense" that they should still be happy in them, and this can include forcing themselves to stay in one location when their souls would be better-served elsewhere. If you are unhappy where you are, stop trying to force yourself to feel otherwise. Instead, allow your feelings of restlessness to speak to you, and then, if needed, plan an excursion for the sake of variety or an exploratory adventure to look into the possibility of relocation. Remember, Great Snowy Owl *must* travel to nourish itself sufficiently, so this is not just about "having fun" but about meeting legitimate emotional, spiritual, and possibly even physical needs.

- If you are feeling cranky, depressed, or lethargic, ask yourself how much sunshine you've gotten lately. If the answer is "very little" or "less than usual," it may be time to amp up the vitamin D in your system! If you are able to get out into the sunshine, do it, even if it means taking a little vacation. On the other hand, if there isn't any sunshine to be had, if you are unable to take a vacation, or if you live in an area in which it is too cold to be outside regardless of the amount of sunlight, talk to your naturopath or holistic healer about natural ways to support your system at this time. You can also talk with your physician about adding prescription-strength vitamin D to your health regimen during winter months (Your doctor should perform a blood test to verify that you are experiencing insufficient levels of vitamin D before deciding whether or not a prescription is appropriate).

SCREECH OWL
Additional totem characteristics:

- Despite their name—"screech" owl—most of these owls do not actually screech! Those that claim to have heard a screech owl have most often heard a barn owl, which *does* screech (and quite dramatically). The screech owl's actual vocalizations most often take the form of a soft, cooing trill or a horse-like whinny, and though it has been known to emit some seriously unhappy noises when being handled by rescuers, none of these even remotely approaches the fearsome sound that so many people have incorrectly assumed to be made by this owl. So how did the screech owl get its name? There does not seem to be a consensus. However, several sources I encountered suggested that the name came from the sound *humans* made (a screech) when startled by the owl's ghostly trill as it perched in the trees near a campfire, waiting to dive after any insects attracted to the light.

Ironically, while the screech owl does not actually make the blood-curdling scream most often attributed to it, this is one of those delightful examples of something being named in a way that reflects its true nature rather than its physical appearance. Screech owls are fiercely aggressive for their size, and they will eat any animal that is their own size or smaller (including other birds). This is similar to possessing extraordinarily small hands; those of us who read palms know that the smaller someone's hands, the bigger the dreams they dream for themselves, and the more powerful their personalities. I cannot tell you how many female CEO's I've read, for example, who have these unbelievably teeny, tiny hands! Screech Owl People, just like their totem, are frequently on the small side physically. They may be especially short or thin or small-boned, and they often have small voices to match. But while people often label them "cute" or "harmless" at first glance, this judgment will inevitably have to be revised. There is nothing "cute" or "harmless" about a mature Screech Owl Person who has set their sights on something they want, and they have no qualms about taking down those who make the mistake of underestimating them.

- Screech owls are particularly effective as a control-measure to neutralize the European starling, which is an invasive and often detrimental species. Starlings are the bullies of the bird-world, using their large numbers to gang up on other birds and drive them off or kill them. Yet despite their small size, screech owls have been known to single-handedly drive off entire flocks of these invaders! As a result, it is not uncommon for Screech Owl People to encounter bullies when they are younger, or to feel as though they are being singled out for torment by a group. This is not because the Screech Owl Person is weak, but rather, because they possess an innate strength and power that is frightening to others, and rather than seek to become stronger themselves, others find it easier to attempt to demoralize the Screech Owl Person, bringing them down to their level. These experiences are gifts from the Universe to help the Screech Owl Person learn how to release any fears of victimization and develop the confidence that no can bring them down or stand in their way unless they allow it. And while these experiences are inarguably uncomfortable, they are necessary for the Screech Owl Person to develop the ability to take a stand against the group-mentality. The most dangerous organizations in the world are those whose security is based upon maintaining ignorance; as an Owl, and therefore, as a Revealer of Truth, Screech Owl People have the power to enlighten those imprisoned by these organizations' limiting beliefs and make great changes in the world.

Additional spirit guide messages:

- No matter what anyone may tell you, you have all the power you need to create *whatever* you want. Don't let others' perceptions of your capability limit what you choose to pursue for yourself.

- If you are being bullied, stop looking at the experience as an instance of victimization, and start seeing it instead as an opportunity to stand up for yourself! No matter how small you are, or how insignificant you may feel, you do not have to let anyone push you around. You are far more powerful than you realize! Too, the way people treat us is largely determined by how we feel about ourselves; the more confidence you develop, the more people will *treat* you like a confident individual!

- It may feel as though someone is intruding in your space and trying to take it for themselves. Do not allow them to do this; this is *your space*, and you have a right to it! Assert yourself!

- Screech Owl is the antidote to the group-mentality. What pieces of yourself have you subjugated or denied because you are afraid of what others will think? What part of your truth are you hiding? BE YOURSELF, and know that you are right to do so.

- It is okay to let others in and allow yourself to be emotionally open, as you have the strength to take care of yourself if the need arises. If you allow someone into your heart and then realize that they are not good for you, you can remove them just as easily as you let them in. You are always safe.

10 OWL AS A DREAM SYMBOL

The Basics of Dream Interpretation

Dreams are of far more use in our pursuit of mental, physical, and spiritual wellness than most people realize; they can warn us when we are on a path that is going to lead us someplace we do not want to be, or reassure us when we are uncertain; they can help us understand the ways in which we may be harming ourselves or holding ourselves back from being happy, healthy, and successful; they can show us when we are finally releasing old, limiting ways of being; they can alert us when someone's intentions are other than they seem; they can tell us when to wait and when to act; and they can give us an astoundingly accurate look into our future, sometimes even years in advance! I strongly recommend that people keep a journal of their dreams, as a dream will often provide you with exactly what you need to know—even when you didn't know you needed it!

When it comes to deciphering the meaning behind our dreams, the most important thing to remember is that more often than not, what we see and experience in a dream is of a symbolic nature rather than a literal one. Too, our minds are exceptionally metaphorical and will often use symbols that represent a common turn of phrase, and so it is best to go about interpreting your dreams with an attitude of playfulness and a willingness to think creatively.

To give you an idea of how to do this, here are some examples using the kitchen, a popular symbol in dreams:

- A dream in which we are constantly checking inside a hot oven to see if our meal is done would indicate that we are feeling impatient about a current process, perhaps wondering if it's ever going to be finished at all. We've done all the work—followed our plan (or "recipe") and prepared the "ingredients"—and now we are having to sit and wait for things to "get cooking."

- If the oven is cold, we are probably feeling like no matter what we do to get things started, nothing is working; in essence, we can't seem to "light a fire" under the process! This dream often occurs for women who are having trouble getting pregnant; they want a "bun in their oven", but can't seem to get their body— the "oven"—to cooperate!

- Stirring a pot of soup or stew on the stove can indicate that we are ruminating or "stewing" over something, or that we are attempting to "stir things up" in a life that is feeling stagnant.

- If we open the refrigerator and find it empty, it may mean that our life feels empty of the things we need to "nourish" ourselves, or that we are afraid that we are living "hand-to-mouth" and don't have the resources we need to survive in an emergency.

- If the fridge is full of food that is spoiling, we may feel that while our life *should* be fun and exciting, it just doesn't contain the things that we really need to feel happy and satisfied—the things that would really "feed" our spirits—and so we feel that our life is "going to waste."

- A fridge full of rotting food can also mean that we feel we are being "spoiled rotten." Someone may be giving us way more than we actually need, and we are unable to make use of it all. How we feel when we see the food spoiling in our dream represents how we feel about being spoiled.

- Because water represents the state of our emotions, if the kitchen sink is broken, we may feel that we are having to bottle up all of our feelings, because we cannot find the right means to express them, or because we simply feel *unable* to express them. We may also feel unable to "wash away" old pain or trauma.

- The kitchen itself also has an overarching meaning. It represents our present degree of creative satisfaction and productivity, our perceived level of safety and security, the degree to which we feel nurtured, the degree to which we feel able to nurture others, and whether or not we feel that we have the power to bring new, fun, and interesting things into our lives—or are totally lacking the necessary "ingredients." When we dream of something happening in the kitchen, it may even represent "food for thought", a notion or idea that it would be in our best interests to reflect upon.

With this in mind, in addition to interpreting the presence of Owl itself, you can greatly improve your ability to "get the message" from your subconscious by exploring the other settings and symbols in your dream and asking yourself what each of these might mean. If you need help doing so, there are some wonderful dream dictionaries out there (and I suggest that you purchase more than one, because many symbols have multiple interpretations that can only be discovered by researching several different sources), or you can contact a professional dream-interpreter like myself. Just remember to always, *always*, **always** write down a significant dream the moment you wake up. I can't tell you how many times I've had an especially vivid dream in the middle of the night, assumed that of *course* I would remember it, because it was so incredible . . . and then forgotten it entirely by morning!

Interpreting Owl as a Dream Symbol
Just as it does as a totem and a spirit guide, when Owl

appears in our dreams, its purpose is usually to encourage us to look at a truth we have been avoiding. More often than not, that "truth" is going to fall into one of the following categories:

Relationships:

- If you are in a romantic relationship, has your gut been telling you that the other person is lying or otherwise concealing something from you? Do you feel that they are saying one thing, but they actually feel something else (such as when someone says, "I love you," but it feels empty, or "Everything's fine," but it still feels like something is wrong)? Are their actions not lining up with their words, or are they continuously making promises they fail to keep? When another person appears in a dream in which Owl is also featured, the dream is often telling us to look specifically at our relationship with that person. Owl would suggest that your romantic partner is hiding something from you, or that they are refusing to face an important truth about themselves. When this is the case, Owl is trying to let us know that the other person's denial about what is occurring in or around them is probably going to start impacting us as well. Whether they are lying to us or lying to themselves, the message is the same: the truth must come out. It may be painful, and it may create uncomfortable changes, but this will still be better for us in the long run than continuing to live in the dark. However, other people in our dreams can represent aspects of ourselves, so if you do not feel that something is awry in your relationship, see the section

137

Personality Facets below.

- If you are in a romantic relationship in which you have lost interest, but you are forcing yourself to stay, a dream about Owl would be asking you to look at the truth of how you really feel. We are never meant to stay in situations that make us unhappy; when we do this, not only are we holding ourselves back and keeping ourselves miserable, but those involved with us can sense these emotions and will be affected by them. Staying in a relationship because you think it's the "right" thing to do can create a lot of resentment, and so what your partner is likely to be feeling from you is not love, but your unhappiness at feeling "stuck" with them. If you really care about your partner, take a good look at how you truly feel; either your attitude needs to change, or you need to set yourself free. Similarly, if you are only staying in the relationship for the security that you believe it offers, Owl would be telling you to look at why you feel you are so powerless. Why do you think you are unable to take care of yourself? Do you feel like a victim? If this is the case, it is time for you to examine your beliefs, begin letting the limiting ones go, and take ownership of your life.

- If your dream about Owl contains another person such as a friend or family member, the same wisdom applies as when we dream about a romantic partner—it is likely that they are somehow failing to be entirely truthful with us or with themselves. However, this is also a case in which the other person may represent an aspect of ourselves and not actually have anything to do with the real person at all, so if you haven't felt any suspicions whatsoever about the person, see the section on *Personality Facets* below.

- If you are a parent and have been feeling as though one of or your children has been up to something they shouldn't be—and most especially if the child appears in the dream—it's time to talk to them directly about your suspicions. Owl is a more urgent messenger than most, and owls are extremely protective parents; if it is appearing in your dream with regard to your children, then you are being strongly urged to make sure that you are really aware of what is going on with them, and that you are paying attention to their safety. At the same time, our children, too, can sometimes represent an aspect of ourselves, and so if you do not feel that anything is amiss with your children, see the section on *Personality Facets* below.

Career/Large Purchase/Paid Service Situations

- When Owl appears in a dream that somehow reminds us of our job or how we *feel* at our job (such as when we dream we are in prison [if our job feels confining or that we aren't able to leave] or when we dream that we are being eaten alive by wild animals [if our boss or coworkers are always "eating us alive" with demands or criticism]), Owl is usually trying to get us to look at how we *really* feel about our work. Because most of us depend upon our jobs for our income, and therefore our survival, it can be especially difficult to admit to ourselves when we are unhappy about how we are presently earning our living. If Owl shows up in a job-related dream, it's time to be honest with yourself. How do you *really* feel about the way you earn your living? If you don't like it, why aren't you leaving? Are you afraid you'll never get another job? Are you afraid that it isn't possible to make a living doing what you *really* want to do? Do you feel like leaving now would be a waste, since you invested so much time in learning to do that job or in working for that company? Perhaps the issue is your boss or coworkers, but you haven't done anything to improve your relationship with them (or filed an outright complaint about them), because you feel powerless, and as though no one would take you seriously (or that you would get fired!).

If you really want to leave and feel that you can't, it's time to take a good look at all the beliefs that are keeping you stuck, begin *feeling* the emotions around them so you can understand why you believe what you do, and then let them go. This will allow you to connect with a way of making a living that is *truly* satisfying for you on all levels. However, if you ask yourself how you really feel about your job and realize that you want to stick with it, and that you would do so happily if some things changed, then it's time to employ some of that Owl flexibility and ask yourself where you can bend a little. Maybe your job would let you make some changes to your hours, maybe you could work under a different boss, or maybe you could explore some different responsibilities. Maybe you could even work from home part (or all!) of the time, if you wanted. You won't know unless you ask.

- When Owl appears in a dream that reminds us of our job, it can also mean that we are ignoring something important that is occurring there. Perhaps we are noticing indicators that the company is about to go out of business or that we are about to be laid off, but we do not want to acknowledge these, because it feels easier to stay in denial. Perhaps there is something immoral or illegal going on, and we are either pretending that we are not aware of it, or have been asked outright not to say anything. Owl tells us that it is *always* better to confront the truth head-on. If you have been feeling like you are about to lose your job, look for other employment options so that you will be ready if this comes to pass. And if you are aware that something is happening that would be detrimental to the health of the company if it came for light, Owl is warning you that the truth is probably going to come out sooner or later. You may need to be the whistle-blower here, or to quit in order to avoid being caught up in the fallout. Trust your intuition to tell you what to do.

- If you are planning to make a large purchase such as a house, a car, a college education, or an expensive trip, and Owl shows up in a dream that features any of these items (or the dream somehow reminds you of these things), you need to put the brakes on your purchase and tune into your gut feelings. In these cases, you have usually felt some discomfort or hesitation about these purchases, or a million little things seem to be going wrong in the pursuit of them, but you've continued to push forward because guilt, fear, or logic have told you that you "should." It is also possible that there is some fine print that you have missed, and the purchase would demand far more payment or commitment from you than you anticipated.

- If you are planning to hire someone to do a job or perform a service for you—whether this is a wedding planner, house-painter, plumber, landscaper, personal assistant, dog-walker, or any other professional—and something that reminds you of this person or the situation to which they are related appears in the same dream as Owl, it is again time to stop, read the fine print, and listen to your gut. If you feel that something may be off about this person or what they are promising to do for you, listen to that feeling, no matter how good their references are!

Health

- If you have noticed that you are not feeling well, or there has been a physical change in your body that frightens you, a dream about Owl that includes elements of your health situation may be telling you that it is time to be brave and see a physician or healer to help you understand what is going on. Not every ailment requires a visit to a health practitioner; in many cases, even when we notice something is wrong with us, we feel a sense of serenity about it, and we know that if we are meant to seek help, we will feel like doing so. Many things simply resolve on their own. If we have been feeling uneasy about our health, however, and part of us knows we should see a doctor or healer but we are afraid to do so, Owl is telling us we need to move through the fear and get a professional opinion. Remaining in denial is not going to help, and may even make things worse.

- If you have been listening to someone else's guidance about your health, and yet it just doesn't feel right to you, an Owl dream that includes elements of your health situation is telling you to listen to YOU, not the other person/ health professional/ media outlet/ trainer/guru/whomever. For example, if you have been juicing religiously because someone told you that that was how they attained "perfect health", but you find that juicing leaves you with an upset stomach and a cranky attitude and you'd really like to quit doing it, Owl would be saying to listen to yourself and quit! If you remain open to doing what is really right for *you*, you will be guided to those things that will truly benefit you.

- Similarly, if you are continuing to do something for your health that is no longer working, or that is actually making you feel sick, but you are doing it because it worked before, or because logic tells you that it "should", an Owl dream at this time would be telling you that you need to listen to your body, *not* your mind. Our bodies are dynamic machines whose needs are always changing, and routines that worked for years may suddenly cease to benefit us and need to be altered. If you listen to your body and remain open to guidance, you will know what to do.

Detail Fixation

- Many of us become stuck in unhappy situations, because we have deliberate ideas about what needs to happen in order for them to change, or for us to let go of the situation entirely and move forward. We think that we can only be happy if *this* thing happens, or *that* thing changes. I must have met a hundred people who have told me that the only way they can be happy is if they win the lottery! Then there are those who insist that they cannot possibly move on from a betrayal until the other person apologizes. When Owl appears in our dreams, it is often telling us that we have become unhealthily fixated upon certain details of our situation, and that our fixation is keeping us stuck. We need to look at the whole picture, at the real truth of the matter! It is not the absence of a lottery win that is keeping us from being happy—it is that we think that we must suffer to have the money that we want. Instead of winning the lottery, we could find or create a job that makes us deliriously happy, meets every single one of our needs, and is so enjoyable that it never feels like we are working. Likewise, it is not someone's refusal to apologize that is keeping us from moving on after a betrayal, but our own need to see them humbled. We can be the bigger person and just let it go; the only one we are hurting by refusing to forgive and move on is *us* anyway!

Emotional Repression

- When we refuse to acknowledge how we are really feeling, we are unable to identify what we really need, we have trouble connecting with the people and experiences that will help us, and we often find ourselves in situations where we feel stuck, frustrated, or victimized. In some cases, we have been in denial of our true feelings about something for so long that we have effectively become numb to them; in other words, we are *so used* to feeling anxious, depressed, frustrated, guilty, sad, etc. that feeling this way seems normal to us, and we've lost touch with the possibility of feeling any other way. This is often when Owl chooses to make an appearance in our dreams, to get us to recognize that we are not supposed to feel like this, and to encourage us to take a good look at those emotions so that we can hear what they are trying to tell us! If Owl shows up in your dreams and you recognize that you've just "gotten used to" feeling a certain way, or that you've convinced yourself that it's not possible for you to feel better, your Higher Self is telling you that this is far from the case. Stop repressing, gather your courage, and start *LISTENING* to those feelings!

Personality Facets

When other people appear in our dreams, the dream often has nothing to do with the person themselves, but with a facet of our personality. People in our lives become symbols for the different parts of ourselves, and so when we encounter them in our dreams, we are being given the opportunity to see how all the different pieces of ourselves work together, which parts need more love and acknowledgement, and which parts need to be released. When Owl appears in a dream with another person, and we haven't been experiencing any underlying feelings that that person might somehow be deceiving us or otherwise being less than truthful, Owl is often trying to get us to look at a particular part of ourselves and how that part is influencing our overall wellness (or lack thereof!).

Following are some of the most common facets of our personalities that appear in dreams:

- *The Wise Teacher*: This individual may appear in the form of a grandmother or grandfather, a teacher, spiritual leader, or anyone else whom we revere for their knowledge and wisdom. This person normally acts as the representative of our Higher Self, the part of us that is always attuned to Divine Guidance and can tell us exactly what to do to move through a current trial or begin the next part of our spiritual journey.

- *The Mother/Nurturer*: This individual often appears in the form of our mother or grandmother, aunt, older sister, or whomever else provided motherly love when we were growing up (and if no one did this for us, then our subconscious might choose a popular social figure, or someone from books or television whom we'd wished could have given us this kind of love). This person typically shows us the degree to which we are— or are not—loving and nurturing ourselves, as well as the degree to which we feel deserving of love and nurturing from others.

- *The Father/Protector.* This individual often appears in the form of our father, older brother, a law-enforcement officer, military serviceman, or whomever else we saw as being our protector (and if no one did this for us, then our subconscious may choose a popular social figure, or someone from books or television whom we'd wished could have been there to protect us). This person represents the degree to which we are honoring our boundaries and saying "NO" when we need to. They can also represent the degree to which we feel safe and secure in our present environment.

- *The Inner Child.* This part of ourselves often appears as one of our children. If we do not have children, a younger version of ourselves, a child we know, or a child we've never seen before may appear here. In some cases, the inner child may even appear as a baby animal, such as a kitten or puppy. The inner child most often calls our attention to childhood wounds that we have not healed. How are we still stuck at the level of a child? Are we still feeling abandonment or a lack of trust in the world, because we were abandoned physically or emotionally as children? Do we feel that we are not allowed to be ourselves, because we were rejected for being ourselves when we were young? The inner child may also appear to show us that we are taking ourselves too seriously and not allowing sufficient fun and play into our day.

- *The Ideal:* This individual most often appears as someone we envy or someone who inspires us, whether this is a real person, or a figure in books, movies, or television. This person shows us what we are really wanting in our lives at this time, what we feel we truly need to be happy and fulfilled. They may also point out the ways that we are criticizing ourselves or labeling ourselves "not good enough."

- *The Guilt-monger:* The guilt-monger most often takes the form of a person in our life who frequently made us feel badly about ourselves and our behavior (this facet of our personality also may also appear as a religious authority, if we were raised in a religious household). This person is the representation of our ego's belief that if we make ourselves feel sufficiently guilty about something, we will never do it again. Through the guilt-monger, we can see the degree to which are able to be flexible and listen to our heart on a day-to-day basis, versus how often we feel like we must abide by certain rules in order to think of ourselves as good people.

- *The Punisher:* The punisher generally takes the form of

the person or being we fear the most. Sometimes this is a parent, sometimes a law-enforcement official or judge, sometimes the Biblical Devil, or someone else whom we perceive as having the power to hurt or control us. When this person appears, we have gone beyond guilt into profound shame and fear; this is the point at which we often begin creating accidents or illnesses as a way of punishing ourselves for a perceived transgression. This is a serious message from our subconscious that we need to be more compassionate with and forgiving of ourselves.

What if YOU Are the Owl in Your Dream?

- If you felt happy or at peace as the Owl, this is often your Higher Self saying: "The truth will set you free!" Whatever you have been afraid to face, if you do so, you are likely to be very pleased with the results. Too, if you have been asking for guidance around whether or not you should pursue a career as a teacher, counselor, or healer, this would be a strong affirmation.

- Feeling particularly happy as the Owl in your dream can also indicate that you have been struggling with setting boundaries or taking time to yourself. Owl is telling you to be more Owl-like and guard your emotional and physical space, as well as your time.

- If you felt unhappy or anxious as the Owl, you may feel that others are rejecting you for being so clear-sighted, and that they would rather that you simply kept your observations to yourself and pretended that everything was okay. You may also wish that you *didn't* know the truth about someone or something or fear what will happen if you speak up.

- If you felt unhappy or anxious, it may also be that you fear that people will reject you for setting boundaries and taking time for yourself.

- If you were in a cage, you may feel that you have been punished for seeing or speaking the truth about someone or something, or that you are not being given a *chance* to speak the truth. You feel stuck.

- If you were unable to fly, you may be feeling that you want to be seen as wise and knowing, or that you wish to pursue the path of a counselor, healer, or teacher, but you just can't seem to get started—to "get your journey off the ground." You may also feel that people do not take you seriously.

The White Owl

- When a white creature appears in our dreams, it most often represents the Divine, the great All-Knowing Force of Creation that exists both *for* us and *IS* us. The Divine knows precisely who and what we are intended to be, what must be done to help or heal us, and how we can become our most loved and loving self. Given that Owl represents Truth, a white Owl is an extremely powerful message that we *need* to look at a truth we have been refusing to acknowledge, because not doing so is preventing us from becoming who we are meant to be. This is a serious, not-to-be-ignored call to transform our lives and become our authentic selves. And because Owl is associated with the night-time and therefore with darkness and our Shadow, this often means we must take a good look at the "darker" parts of ourselves that we have been ignoring, because they frighten or embarrass us. If we are already doing this—examining our Shadow and lovingly confronting those truths we have previously refused to acknowledge—the white Owl can also be taken as a sign of affirmation from the Universe that you are on the right track, and that continuing to do this will lead to feeling a new sense of joy and freedom.

JORDANA VAN

11 LOOKING DEEPER: A VISIT FROM GREAT SNOWY OWL WOMAN

While we often encounter our totems and guides in "real" life, they can indeed come to us in the form of visions or dreams. Below is a precise recounting of the way in which Great Snowy Owl came to me when I was ill and told me how to heal. It remains one of the most magical events of my life.

I had been in constant pain for nearly a year-and-a-half when, on top of the preexisting discomfort, I developed another. My left breast suddenly began to hurt so badly that I could only think I must have developed cancer, and my left side and underarm were on fire. I was beyond exhausted and feeling that same malaise one experiences right before one develops a cold.

But as I said, I'd been in pain for a very, very long time, and so this wasn't anything earth-shattering. Pain had become a way of life at this point, and I'd been to dozens of doctors who told me that not only was there absolutely nothing wrong with me, but that I was actually in flawless good health! Except for the pain, of course, which they weren't able to explain. I'd been to dozens of healers, too, as well as a few shamans, and I had spent more money than I earned in a year. Yet at the end of the day, there were no answers, the pain would intensify and lessen seemingly on its own schedule, and there didn't seem to be a thing I could do about it.

But this pain in my breast . . . this was new. And it was a different kind of pain than what I had been experiencing up to this point, a hot, sharp agony unlike the aching tension that had lived in my neck, chest, jaw, and shoulders for so long.

I didn't know it at the time, but I was approximately three hours away from developing such an intense outbreak of shingles that when I arrived at Urgent Care a few days later, the nurse's jaw dropped in shock.

My best friend was visiting, and we'd filled the day with wandering my favorite art fair, shopping at some vintage stores, cooking, eating, laughing, reminiscing, and otherwise having a ball. I was having a delightful time except for the pain, but shortly before we were supposed to go out to dinner that night, I hit a wall. My body literally refused to keep me upright any longer, and I knew I had to lie down and meditate. I had been meditating like crazy on Pain Number One with almost no success, and I was terrified that meditating on this new pain would yield only silence as well. But I didn't seem to have any other option.

So I went into our bedroom, turned off the lights and lay down. My eyes had begun to burn with exhaustion at this point, and I was feeling the teasing edge of a fever, but

I closed my eyes and repeated my meditation mantra, "I am just going to listen," over and over again until I felt my body begin to fall. There was a jerk and the sensation of landing, and I was standing out in the open beneath a black sky pulsating with millions of stars. Soft dirt, pleasantly dry and gritty, tickled my bare feet, and the distinct pop and snap of a fire crackled in my ears. I could feel its warmth on my skin, and no sooner did I realize this than a bonfire came into view, and beside it, an old, Native American woman. I could feel her warmth, too, as unmistakable as the heat from the flames next to which she stood. She was wearing a hood and cloak of snowy owl feathers, her adobe-colored hand raised to beckon gently. Though I could see nothing of her face but the partial curve of her smile, and though she did not speak, I knew that I was supposed to join her beneath her cloak. But as I stepped forward to do so, the pain intensified and jarred me out of the vision. Tears stung my eyes, but not from the pain. I knew I had just been given a huge gift, but I had no idea what it was!

I'd been reading about animal guides for awhile at this point, and yet nothing I had learned about Owl's wisdom seemed to apply to my situation. If such a thing was possible, I felt more dejected and afraid than I had before I'd received the vision, since what was the use of a vision if I didn't know how to interpret it?

Ten minutes later, I was in the bathroom trying to pull myself together to go to dinner when I saw it—a huge, angry swath of blisters on the underside of my left breast and below my left armpit. I had never experienced shingles before, and so I just assumed it was a particularly nasty rash and asked myself what I knew about the emotional causes of skin eruptions such as this one. Some of the wisdom fit and some didn't, but I was in a hurry, I was worn out and sick of trying to figure out why I was sick, and so I told myself I just wasn't going to think about it until tomorrow. It hurt, but so what? I was always hurting these days. We went to dinner, took my friend to the airport, and when my husband I got home, we curled up in front of the T.V. to wind down a bit before going to bed. We love nature shows, so it wasn't a shock to find the television already tuned to one. What *was* a surprise was that the station was showing a documentary about owls. Great snowy owls, to be exact.

We had turned it on during the section about how great snowy owls hunt, and how their hearing is so acute that they can detect and seize their prey up to ten inches under the snow. Nothing can hide from a great snowy owl! I didn't know why this mattered, but something inside me told me that it *did*.

Three days later, my guides told me it was time to go to the doctor, and I was given a diagnosis of shingles. Now I knew what Great Snowy Owl Woman was telling me! Shingles is most often caused by refusing to forgive those who have wounded us, and I most definitely had some forgiveness-work to do! Just before the original pain started, I experienced two massive betrayals that dwarfed anything I had ever experienced before. They were so intense that I simply went numb, unable to be angry, unable to be sad, unable to be . . . anything. Those two episodes were so intense that I didn't even know where to begin feeling pain, and so I didn't feel anything at all. But that didn't mean those emotions were gone; I'd simply stuffed them down beneath the level of conscious access. Day after day, I would think about these betrayals and wonder why these people had hurt me, and day after day, the emotions continued to fester beneath the surface of my psyche.

My body was telling me that it was time to feel again, and through feeling, to begin to release and heal. Using what I had learned about great snowy owls from the documentary, as well as my vision in which Great Snowy Owl Woman wanted me to join her under her cloak, I was able to determine what needed to be done: I needed to become a great snowy owl myself and dive beneath the snow to obtain my prize. Water is the element that represents our emotions, and snow, being water that has frozen, is indicative of emotional numbness. If I was going to get rid of the shingles, I was going to need to break through that numbness and finally begin to *feel* something about those betrayals.

And so for several hours a day for the next five days, I would retreat to our guest room with a pen, my notebook, and a box of tissues, and I would do active visualizations in which I would tell the two people who had wounded me everything I would have told them if I knew that they could—and would—hear me. The more I did this, the more real the visions became, and finally, those to whom I was speaking began to speak in turn. When I emerged from the visions, I would usually cry for awhile (which was difficult at first, since I had not cried in many years, yet another representation of a way in which I had been "frozen"), then I would write down what had occurred along with any questions or feelings I still had at the time.

Five days later, the visions were becoming shorter and less intense, and there wasn't as much to write. The original pain remained, but the pain from the shingles had vanished, along with the blisters, which had not scarred.

Having not even realized how clogged with emotional wounds my body had become, I felt clean for the first time since the betrayals had occurred. I no longer felt confused, nor hurt or angry, and it was not because I was numb, but rather, because I had come to terms with what had happened and let it go. The pain that had crystallized inside me had been melted with the warmth of forgiveness, and so there was no longer any need for shingles to tell me there was a problem. The problem was gone.

A week after my diagnosis, there wasn't a scrap of evidence to suggest I'd ever experienced shingles, and the lingering effects I'd been warned to expect—continued outbreaks, scarring, intense nerve pain—never made an appearance. Through the wisdom of Great Snowy Owl, I had healed myself in record time.

As for the pain that pre-dated the outbreak of shingles, it, too, eventually began to unravel with the aid of Great Snowy Owl, who continued to gently remind me that the source of all pain lies within, and that the only path to healing lay in allowing myself to experience the fear, grief, shame, and anger that I had repressed. The more I allowed myself to feel, the more I saw the truth of who I really was and who I was intended to be, and the more the fears that had dominated my life until that point gradually lost their terror. When we are no longer afraid, we are no longer limited in our ability to dream big dreams for ourselves, and we no longer struggle to make those dreams a reality. In a life filled with countless spiritual blessings, this is the one for which I am the most grateful: undeniable evidence that we are the creators of our own experience, and that all we must do to achieve mental, physical, and spiritual wellness is accept ourselves for precisely who we are.

JORDANA VAN

Bibliography

Electronic

"Adaptations_Catching Prey." *Project BEAK.* Web. 30 June 2016.
<http://projectbeak.org/adaptations/feet_catching.htm>.

"All About Owl Pellets." *All About Owl Pellets.* Web. 5 Jan. 2015. <http://www.carolina.com/teacher-resources/Interactive/basic-information-on-owl-pellets/tr11103.tr>.

"Barn Owl." *All About Birds.* Web. 6 Jan. 2015. <http://www.allaboutbirds.org/guide/Barn_Owl/lifehistory>.

"Barn Owl Adaptations." *The Barn Owl Trust.* Web. 2 Aug. 2016. <http://www.barnowltrust.uk/barn-owl-facts/barn-owl-adaptations>.

"Barred Owl – Strix Varia." *Island Creeks Ecology.* Web. 12 Aug. 2016. <http://www.fcps.edu/islandcreekes/ecology/barred_owl.htm>.

"Barred Owl – strix varia." *Study of Northern Virginia Ecology.* Web. 2 Aug. 2016. <http://www.fcps.edu/islandcreekes/ecology/barred_owl.htm>.

"Birding Information – Great Horned Owl." *Birding Information.* Web. 12 Aug. 2016. <http://www.birdinginformation.com/birds/owls/great-horned-owl/>.

"Beaks, Feathers and Flight." *World of Owls.* Web. 5 July 2016. <http://www.worldofowls.com/beaks-feathers-and-flight/>.

"Burrowing Owl." *National Wildlife Federation.* Web. 23 June 2016. <https://www.nwf.org/Wildlife/Wildlife-Library/Birds/Burrowing-Owl.aspx>.

"Burrowing Owl." *The Cornell Lab of Ornithology_All About*

Birds. Web. 23 June 2016.
    <https://www.allaboutbirds.org/guide/Burrowing_Owl
    /id>.

"Burrowing Owl (Athene Cunicularia)." *Wildscreen Arkive.*
    Web. June 23 2016.
    <http://www.arkive.org/burrowing-owl/athene-
    cunicularia/>.

Cantrel, J. (2004). "Bubo Bubo." *Animal Diversity Web.*
    Web. 12 Aug. 2016.
    <http://animaldiversity.org/accounts/Bubo_bubo/>.

"Common Barn Owl." *Rosamond Gifford Zoo.* Web. 2 Aug.
    2016.
    <http://rosamondgiffordzoo.org/assets/uploads/anim
    als/pdf/CommonBarnOwl.pdf>.

Cudmore, Becca (9 Feb. 2015). "No, Barred Owls are Not
    Trying to Kill You." *Audubon.* Web. 6 Aug. 2016.
    <http://www.audubon.org/news/no-barred-owls-are-
    not-trying-kill-you>.

"Digestive System of Great Horned Owl." *The Great Horned
    Owl Resource.* Web. 30 June 2016.
    <http://greathornedowlresource.weebly.com/digestive-
    system.html>.

"Eastern Screech Owl (Megascops Asio)." *Owl Research
    Institute.* Web. 3 Aug. 2016.
    <http://www.owlinstitute.org/eastern-screech-
    owl.html>.

"Eurasian Eagle-Owl." *The National Aviary.* Web. 6 Jan.
    2015. <http://www.aviary.org/animals/eurasian-eagle-
    owl>.

"Eurasian Eagle-Owl—Bubo Bubo." *The Owl Pages.* Web.
    6 Aug. 2016.
    <http://www.owlpages.com/owls/species.php?s=1240
    >.

"Eurasian Eagle-Owl (Bubo Bubo)." *Wildscreen Arkive.*
    Web. 6 Aug. 2016. <http://www.arkive.org/eurasian-
    eagle-owl/bubo-bubo/>.

"Food and Hunting." *World of Owls.* Web. June 24 2016. < http://www.worldofowls.com/food-and-hunting/>.

Frost, Paul D. "Eurasian Eagle Owl (Bubo Bubo)." *Raptors.* Web. 8 Aug. 2016. <http://www.pauldfrost.co.uk/eeagleowl.html>.

Frost, Paul D. "Little Owl (Athene Noctua)." *Raptors.* Web. 5 Jan. 2015. <http://www.pauldfrost.co.uk/littleowl.html>.

Frost, Paul D. "Owl Introduction." *Raptors.* Web. 24 June 2016. < http://www.pauldfrost.co.uk/intro_o.html>.

"Flying Team." *International Centre of Birds of Prey Worldwide Conservation.* Web. 8 Aug. 2016. <http://www.icbp.org/index/index.php/about-6/flying-team>.

"Great Grey Owl." *The Nature Conservatory.* Web. 22 June 2016. <http://www.nature.org/newsfeatures/specialfeatures/animals/birds/great-grey-owl.xml>.

"Great Horned Owl." *All About Birds, Life History.* Web. 6 Jan. 2015. <http://www.allaboutbirds.org/guide/great_horned_owl/lifehistory>.

"Great Horned Owls, Great Horned Owl Pictures, Great Horned Owl Facts." *National Geographic.* Web. 6 Jan. 2015. <http://animals.nationalgeographic.com/animals/birds/great-horned-owl/>."

"Kinds of Owls." *The Aviary at Owls.com.* Web. 11 Jan. 2015. <http://aviary.owls.com/owls.html>.

Lee, Carol (26 Mar. 2006). "Powerful Feet and Talons Help Birds of Prey Make Their Living." *Lubbock Avalanche-Journal.* Web. 5 July 2016. <http://lubbockonline.com/stories/032606/gue_032606062.shtml#.V3wCH7n6tdh>.

Lewis, Deane. "Barred Owl – Strix Varia." *The Owl Pages.* Web. 2 Aug. 2016.

<http://www.owlpages.com/owls/species.php?s=1740>.

Lewis, Deane (30 Nov. 2015). "Burrowing Owl – Athene Cunicularia." *The Owl Pages.* Web. June 23 2016. <http://www.owlpages.com/owls/species.php?s=2250>.

Lewis, Deane (19 Jan. 2016). "Owl Ears and Hearing." *The Owl Pages.* Web. 30 June 2016. <http://www.owlpages.com/owls/articles.php?a=6>.

Lewis, Deane (1 July 2015). "Owl Feet and Talons." *The Owl Pages.* Web. 30 June 2016. <http://www.owlpages.com/owls/articles.php?a=9>.

Lewis, Deane. "Owl Articles - Owl Physiology - The Owl Pages." *The Owl Pages.* Web. 6 Aug. 2014. <http://www.owlpages.com/articles.php?section=Owl Physiology&title=Reproduction>.

Mayntz, Melissa. "20 Fun Facts About Owls - Owl Trivia." *About.com.* Web. 11 Jan. 2015. <http://birding.about.com/od/birdprofiles/a/20-Fun-Facts-About-Owls.htm>.

McKitrick, Mary (27 Aug. 2010). "Avian Bloopers: My Cousin Vinny." *Mary McKitrick Voiceovers.* Web. 6 Aug. 2016. <http://www.marymckitrick.com/blog/?p=662>.

Mythili, Mysore. "Why Is the Owl Considered a Wise Bird in the West and a Symbol of Foolishness in India?" *The Times of India.* Web. 5 Jan. 2015. <http://timesofindia.indiatimes.com/home/stoi/Why-is-the-owl-considered-a-wise-bird-in-the-West-and-a-symbol-of-foolishness-in India/articleshow/871894.cms>.

"Meet the Birds." *Feather Perfect Falconry.* Web. 8 Aug. 2016. <http://www.featherperfect.co.uk/meet-the-team/>.

"Native American Totems and Their Meanings." *Legends of America.* Web. 12 Jan. 2015.

<http://www.legendsofamerica.com/na-totems.html>.

"Nature Notes - Barn Owl." *Barn Owl.* Web. 7 Jan. 2015. <http://www.alicespringsdesertpark.com.au/kids/natur e/birds/owl.shtml>.

Nicholson, Amanda (13 Mar. 2013). "Wildlife Classroom Series: Owl Eyes." *The Wildlife Center of Virginia.* Web. 4 July 2017. <http://wildlifecenter.org/sites/default/files/pdfs/wcc s%20owl%20/Eyes%20031313.pdf>.

Osborne, Tim (1994). "Great Gray Owl." *Alaska Department of Fish and Game.* Web. 22 June 2016. <https://www.adfg.alaska.gov/static/education/wns/gr eat_gray_owl.pdf>.

"Owl Articles - Owl Physiology - The Owl Pages." *The Owl Pages.* Web. 5 Jan. 2015. <http://www.owlpages.com/articles.php?section=Owl Physiology&title=Vision>.

"Owl Mystery Unraveled: Scientists Explain How Bird Can Rotate its Head without Cutting off Blood Supply to Brain." *ScienceDaily.* Web. 7 Aug. 2014. <http://www.sciencedaily.com/releases/2013/01/1301 31144102.htm>.

"Snowy Owl." *All About Birds, Identification.* Web. 7 Jan. 2015. <http://www.allaboutbirds.org/guide/snowy_owl/id>.

"The Great Gray Owl, Manitoba's Provincial Bird." *Naturenorth.com.* Web. 22 June 2016. <http://www.naturenorth.com/Gray_Owl/Gray_Owl. html>.

"The Barn Owl – Tyto Alba." *Chrissie's Owls.* Web. 2 Aug. 2016. <http://www.chrissiesowls.com/owl- information-barnowl.php>.

Traynor, Robert M. (17 Apr. 2012). "Directional Hearing in Owls." *Hearing Health & Technology Matters.* Web. 30 June 2016. <http://hearinghealthmatters.org/hearinginternational/

2012/directional-hearing-in-owls-robery-m-traynor-ed-d/>.

"Tyto Alba – Barn Owl." *Cincinnati Zoo.* Web 2 Aug. 2016. < http://cincinnatizoo.org/wp-content/uploads/2013/05/Barn-Owl-complete.pdf>.

Warren, Lynne (Feb. 2005). "Great Gray Owls." *National Geographic Magazine.* Web. 22 June 2016. < http://ngm.nationalgeographic.com/ngm/0502/feature4/>.

"Western Screech-Owl." *Bird Web – Seattle Audubon Society.* Web. 3 Aug. 2016. <http://www.seattleaudubon.org/birdweb/bird/western_screech-owl>.

Film & Television

Magic of the Snowy Owl. Dir. Fergus Beeley and Matt Hamilton. PBS, 2012. Television.

My Cousin Vinny. Dir. Johnathan Lynn. Writ. Dale Launer. Twentieth Century Fox Film Corporation, 1992. Film.

Superhuman Animals: Sound. Dir. Kristine Davidson and Sam Hodgson. BBC America, 2014. Television.

Lecture

Grow, Leslie. "The Fast and the Furious." *Raptor Days.* The Dwight Chamberlain Raptor Rehab Center and Friends of Hardy Lake. Hardy Lake, Scottsburg, Indiana. 28 Sept. 2012. Lecture.

Personal Correspondence

Information about screech owls provided by Eileen Wicker, Program Director of Raptor Rehabilitation of Kentucky, Inc., Louisville, Kentucky. Aug. 2016. E-mail.

Information about screech owls provided by Louise
Shimmel, Executive Director of Cascades Raptor
Center, Eugene Oregon. Aug. 2016. E-mail.

Personal account of resonance with Burrowing Owl
provided by Burrowline of Paris, France. June 2016. E-
mail.

Print

Andrews, Ted. *Animal Speak*. Woodbury, MN: Llewellyn
Publications, 2012.

Arroyo, Stephen. *Person-to-Person Astrology: Energy Factors in
Love, Sex & Compatibility*. Berkely, CA: Frog Books,
2007.

Frost, Paul D. *Birds of Prey*. Bath, UK: Parragon
Publishing, 2006.

Hawkins, David R. *Letting Go: The Pathway of Surrender*.
Carlsbad, CA: Hay House, 2014.

Vanner, Michael. *The Encyclopedia of North American Birds*.
Bath, UK: Parragon Publishing, 2003.

JORDANA VAN

ABOUT THE AUTHOR

Jordana Van is a holistic energy healer, metaphysical counselor, writer, and scholar of animal wisdom with a lifetime of education and experience in the fields of energetic healing, natural wellness, astrology, numerology, divination, dream interpretation, animal spiritualism, and metaphysics. She is also the owner of Ravenlight Holistic Healing, L.L.C. and works with individuals worldwide to heal chronic mental and physical illness and foster a loving connection with the Authentic Self.

When she is not quilting, baking, singing folk songs at the top of her lungs, planting something, or out walking or running, she is probably attempting to do yoga without falling over her dog or cat, who like to help.

To learn more about Jordana, or to schedule a private session or speaking-appearance, you can visit her website at www.ravenlightholistichealing.com. Ravenlight Holistic Healing, L.L.C. is also on Facebook and Instagram, and on YouTube, where you can view a large collection of videos Jordana has created about different animal totems and spirit guides.

Made in the USA
Columbia, SC
15 May 2020